Collaborative
Ministry

Collaborative Ministry

Skills and Guidelines

Loughlan Sofield, ST
Carroll Juliano, SHCJ

AVE MARIA PRESS Notre Dame, IN 46556

International Standard Book Number: 0-87793-360-X

Library of Congress Catalog Card Number: 87-70901

Printed and bound in the United States of America.

To our parents

Mary and George Sofield
Eleanor and Jerry Juliano

we dedicate this book in love and gratitude

Acknowledgments

This book is the result of collaboration, not just between the two authors, but with the many friends and colleagues whose gifts helped it to completion.

First, we are deeply grateful to Dr. James Gill, SJ, for his graciousness in writing the Foreword.

We wish to thank those who generously allowed the use of computer equipment: Sister Mary Lawrence Habetz, O.Carm, Mount Carmel Academy, New Orleans, Louisiana; Sister Ruth Dawley, SHCJ, Oak Knoll School, Summit, New Jersey; Sister Annette Meilleur, OSB, Benedictine Priory, Winnipeg, Canada; Brothers James McPike, ST, and Howard Piller, ST, Missionary Servants of the Most Holy Trinity, Silver Spring, Maryland.

We extend a special word of thanks for the editing expertise offered by Sister Marlene Brownett, SHCJ, Joan Rodriquez and Joan Wyatt.

In developing the material for this book, we depended on the good will of many friends who critiqued the manuscript: Hope Crowley; Eleanor Doyle; Donald Doyle; Elizabeth Fitzmaurice, SHCJ; Janet Franklin, CSJ; Janet Hockman, MM; Georgeanna Juliano; Elmer Marquard; Marian Schwab; Malachy Sofield, ST; Mary Sofield; Raymond Sofield; and Elizabeth Stringer, OP.

We are grateful to Rosine Hammett, CSC, who assisted in developing the material in Chapter Seven. We are indebted to Dr. James Tooley of Mobile, Alabama, for the model on burnout used in Chapter Two, and to Community Creativity, Inc., of Washington, DC, for the outline for the graph in Chapter Five.

Finally, we wish to express our appreciation to the many participants who attended our workshops and classes. Their critiques and suggestions were of great assistance in refining our ideas.

Contents

Foreword

When the Lord sent out his disciples on their apostolic missions, he assigned them to work in pairs. It isn't hard to guess why. They were headed for difficulties and failures as well as successes and joys. Mutual support could help them to persevere and grow spiritually through the painful experiences. And the sharing of their toils and struggles, for his sake, could enable them to engage in prayer and labor and celebration in a way that no loner ever can. Jesus knew what he was doing; he knew his disciples' needs.

Perhaps more profoundly, the Master must have intended that those he chose for ministry should work in pairs or larger groups so that they could pool the efforts of their minds and hearts in the pursuit of a deeper and more comprehensive understanding of the Father and his actions. Reflecting together on their experiences in ministry might teach them infinitely more about God and grace than an isolated laborer could ever be expected to discover.

Moreover, different workers bring different gifts into the vineyard. Combining the talents, experience and wisdom God has distributed among those he sends out together in service makes possible a quality and breadth of impact that no solitary minister trying to meet the complex spiritual, moral and other human needs of God's children could ever hope to provide.

Today, no less than in Jesus' time, all these things are true in regard to ministry. The work experience of countless persons, including the authors of this book, gives convincing evidence of the value of collaboration whether measurement is made in terms of assistance to others or personal growth and sense of fulfillment.

But working in teams is not usually easy; differences in expectations, attitudes, needs and maturity give rise to misunderstanding, conflict and hurt feelings all too readily. This book can contribute to greater success in collaborative efforts as well as to diminishing the pains and augmenting the joys.

I doubt that when Jesus sent his disciples into ministry he insisted that they aim at "intimacy" in their relationships. But surely he hoped they would deeply share in mind and heart their ongoing experience of him, and of each other in him. Today's disciples can be helped immensely with this book to guide their interactions.

I believe that all of us contemporary ministers—lay, religious and clergy—need to develop a lifelong mutual disclosure of the Spirit-ignited insights, visions, feelings and strivings that propel us individually. By pooling all these in our ministry, we truly function as one Body, with one life and one mission, namely Christ's.

James J. Gill, SJ, M.D.

Introduction

The Second Vatican Council challenged all Christians with a threefold call to holiness, to ministry and to community. That same council also introduced an integrative context for responding to that triple call, the concept of the People of God. Previously the framework for ministry accented the call of the individual Christian. Now the focus is upon the holiness and ministry of "the people"—a mutual, shared, collaborative approach.

Collaboration, as we define it, is the identification, release and union of the gifts of all baptized persons. The belief that every baptized person is gifted and called to ministry is the basis for collaboration. The concept of giftedness is central to an understanding and implementation of collaborative ministry.

Today's Christians are witnessing and experiencing movement toward a more collaborative church. In responding to the challenge this presents, many ministers realize that their preparation for ministry focused primarily on individual competence. As a result, many individuals and groups (parishes, agencies, teams, institutions) are searching for models and skills to assist them in ministering collaboratively. Recently, in the United States, we have seen a proliferation of national meetings on the topic of collaboration. Central among the issues emerging from these discussions are the need for a common understanding of the meaning of collaboration and the need for resources to assist groups with the processes and skills that are necessary to achieve it.

This book attempts to share insights and observations gleaned from five years of conducting workshops and courses on the topic of collaboration. The purpose of the book is to encourage ministry groups that are working collaboratively and to offer some information, skills and guidelines that can facilitate their efforts. While the book is directed primarily toward those who are in positions to foster and promote collaboration, it is hoped that the material will prove helpful to anyone interested in ministering collaboratively.

No one will move toward collaboration unless there is a basic conviction about its value, so we begin with a discussion of the concept of collaborative ministry and a personal assessment of beliefs. Even if there is a deep conviction, however, there may be obstacles present; Chapter Two covers some of these common obstacles. Other chapters examine individual readiness for collaboration; a spirituality for an apostolic-collaborative lifestyle; and elements to consider in planning for collaboration. Group leadership, conflict and confrontation—important skills required for anyone ministering collaboratively—will be discussed in later chapters. The questions which follow some of the chapters are offered to trigger individual reflection and to stimulate discussion among those who are working toward collaboration.

Collaboration is a growing concept in the church, but it is still very much in the infancy stage. We hope that, in some small way, this book will contribute to the developing understanding and further implementation of collaboration.

Loughlan Sofield, ST
Carroll Juliano, SHCJ

One

Beliefs About Collaborative Ministry

Not long ago a group of priests from a large New England diocese recounted a story about a local pastor:

One Sunday after Mass a parishioner approached the pastor and asked if it would be possible for a woman to serve as lector at the liturgies.

The pastor responded simply and succinctly, "No."

The parishioner then asked if they could discuss the issue.

The pastor replied, "We just did."

While collaborative ministry is often encouraged and fostered, this story dramatizes the frustration occasionally encountered in attempting to implement collaboration in ministry.

The basis for all ministry is giftedness. A person's call to ministry is a direct response to the gifts God has bestowed on that person, and ministry should flow from those gifts. Collaborative ministry brings together various gifts to accomplish the mission of Jesus Christ. The goal of collaboration is to discover ways to identify, release, utilize and unify the gifts of *all* baptized Christians. The 1985 Extraordinary Synod of Bishops affirmed this challenge and exhorted all the faithful to "participation and co-responsibility at all levels."[1] This exhortation is a continuation of the universal invitation to ministry which has always been present in the church, but has become more prominent since the Second Vatican Council.

The concept of collaborative ministry extends beyond the mere incorporation of a specific group, for example, the laity. It is broader than programs which add lectors and eucharistic ministers to the sacramental and liturgical ministries. Implementation of collaborative ministry calls for efforts to enable all Christians to respond to their baptismal call and engage in ministry with others in the Christian community.

A major challenge confronting today's church is the translation of an ideal concept of collaboration into the reality of daily life. How can people of diverse cultures, lay and ordained, women and men, work toward a mutual goal of proclaiming the good news and extending the kingdom? Developing a concept of ministry which encompasses each person involves more than mere recognition and acceptance. It takes work.

In recent history ministry has been placed into the hands of only a small number of the gifted Christian com-

---

[1] Extraordinary Synod of Bishops (1985), "A Message to the People of God," *Origins*, Vol. 15, Dec. 19, 1985, No. 27, p. 449.

munity. The church and Christians in general have viewed ministry almost solely as the responsibility of professed men and women religious, the ordained, and some laity. In addition, ministry formation often fostered a "Lone Ranger" approach to ministry. Yet any significant inroads into eliminating some of the world's most critical issues such as hunger, injustice and poverty will not be accomplished by one person or by a small group. It will require the efforts of many people with differing philosophies, theologies and backgrounds working together to effect attitudinal and structural change. A minister in today's church who conveys an "I can do it alone" attitude makes collaboration impossible and curtails the work of the Lord.

As the focus of responsibility for ministry shifts to a more universal base, the need for re-education and adaptation becomes apparent. The transition is difficult since many ministers were not trained or formed to see collaborative ministry as a value. Collaborative ministry cannot be implemented without explicit, intentional efforts to promote and foster its development.

The ultimate goal of collaboration is always to involve in ministry 100 percent of the baptized, gifted people of God. Movement toward this ideal is accomplished by challenging specific populations and situations within the church:

— men and women, especially priests and women religious, to minister together more harmoniously;

— parish staffs to develop greater collaborative skills and to be models for parishioners of what collaboration is all about;

— chancery and parish staffs to relate to each other as allies rather than adversaries;

— those living in religious communities and rectories to witness ways Christians can live and work together;

— neighboring parishes to combine efforts to meet the needs of suffering people;

— organizations within the same parish to discover ways to work together;

— diocesan agencies to function cooperatively rather than competitively.

Stages in the Development of Collaborative Ministry

The transition from a traditional style of ministry to a more collaborative one is a gradual process. The movement toward implementing collaborative ministry passes through some predictable stages.

Stage I, that of little or no collaboration, is represented by the story of the pastor described in the first paragraph. This stage characterized the church prior to the Second Vatican Council. The hierarchical model of church was devoid of a general understanding of or desire for collaboration, and situations where collaboration was valued and implemented were the exception.

Stage II, the awareness and recognition of collaboration as a value, can lead to an obsession with the rhetoric of collaboration. During this stage inordinate amounts of time and energy are spent discussing or writing about collaboration; heated, often endless, and usually highly intellectual discussions over the language to be used in describing the concept of collaborative ministry are frequent.

While preciseness of language is important in expressing concepts, language can also serve as a form of resistance. Over-involvement in the rhetoric of collaboration may be a way to avoid the difficult process of actually implementing it. Discussions which move the participants to clarity and action are fruitful. However, when action is not a discernible outcome of discussion, it can be assumed that the group is avoiding moving beyond Stage II.

Ambivalence is the mark of *Stage III*. The desire to move toward greater collaboration is coupled with a fear of doing so. Often individuals are not even conscious of the reasons for their resistance. Fears can be many and varied, and often relate to issues of loss and self-esteem. Some fear loss of prestige, power, control or identity. Others may be afraid of the unknown demands which may be placed upon them. Grappling with the pressures of collaboration may give rise to feelings of inadequacy or fear of failure which are threats to self-esteem. Until whatever fears exist are recognized and articulated, it will be virtually impossible to move beyond the stage of ambivalence.

Stage IV is the action stage; energy is channeled toward making collaboration a reality. Individuals and groups invest time, energy and, in some cases, money to accomplish their goal. They remain committed even when their efforts meet with the inevitable frustrations and conflicts.

To summarize:

STAGE	DESCRIPTION	CHARACTERIZED BY
I. No collaboration	Collaboration not a value	Rigid hierarchical model
II. Obsession	Obsession with talking and writing about collaboration	Endless discussion. Articulate documents but little action
III. Ambivalence	Belief in the value of collaboration coupled with fear	Attempts at collaboration but no long-term commitment in the face of difficulties
IV. Action	Commitment to collaboration as an operational norm	Willingness to continue even when it is difficult

The Decisions of Collaboration

In order to arrive at the stage of action, three prior decisions regarding collaboration have to be made. "We should" is the first decision. Exploring and identifying the reasons for the choice is basic if a commitment to work at collaboration is to be realized. Some church ministers may discover that they have not as yet committed themselves to the ideal of collaborative ministry. The commitment must evolve from a belief in the value of collaboration both for the individual and for the church.

The second decision, "We want to," moves beyond the objective reasons for choosing collaboration to the point of personal, conscious ownership of the commitment.

The third decision is "We can." The people who commit themselves to collaboration must believe that they possess the resources to make it a reality. In order to arrive at this decision, individual ministers and ministry groups need to address two areas: Is there the individual willingness and capacity to move in the direction of collaboration? Does the group possess the skills necessary for collaborative ministry?

These three decisions are all necessary elements for the final decision: "We will." Individuals will not move into action unless all the implications of these elements are examined and choices made.

"We Should"

There are two basic reasons why many people believe that collaboration in ministry is essential. For some, the conviction is rooted in their theology. For others, the statistics of declining numbers of full-time ministers have convinced them of the absolute necessity for collaboration.

It is our belief that the ultimate reason for choosing to become collaborative is that the church is the People of God, that every baptized person is both called and gifted for ministry. Ministry, then, is not a choice for the Christian, but a privilege and an obligation. Beyond the individual call for ministry, there is a call as a people. This corporate call implies the necessity for individuals to discover ways to join their gifts with the gifts of others for the building of the kingdom. Avery Dulles describes clearly this concept in speaking of the church as a community of disciples.[2] The goal is to unite these gifted people whose purpose is discipleship and ministry into a community which exists for evangelization. The essence of collaboration is to develop a church in which people continue to discover new and better ways of working together in ministry toward that common mission.

This model contains strong implications for anyone in full-time ministry. Francis Morrisey suggests that the primary role of the pastor is to animate the entire Christian community to assume its role for carrying out the pastoral responsibilities of the church.[3] We believe that this role of animation applies to anyone in full-time pastoral ministry.

For many Christians, especially those who have not yet been moved to action by their theology, the current statistics may provide the impetus for re-evaluating their theological beliefs and deciding to move toward greater collaboration.

During the last decade a plethora of articles has highlighted present statistics about sisters, brothers and priests. The statistics offered are often contradictory; however, some common elements seem to emerge. In First-World countries, and perhaps in some others, the number of priests, sisters and brothers is declining while the median age is rising. This reality can serve as a challenge to the traditional ways of thinking about ministry, especially when the decline is accompanied, as it often is, by an increase in the number and/ or percentage of Catholics in these same countries.

[2] Avery Dulles, "Imaging Church for the 1980s," *Thought*, Vol. 56, June 1981, pp. 121-138.
[3] Francis Morrisey, "Pastors and Parishes According to the New Code of Canon Law," *Pastoral Life*, Vol. 32, No. 5, pp. 2-11.

"We Want To"

Determining the factors that stand in the way of commitment to collaborative ministry requires honest examination and evaluation of our behavior and our experiences in ministry. The next chapter lists some of the obstacles which might prevent commitment from occurring.

"We Can"

Even after there is conviction that "We should" and "We want to" be more collaborative, nothing will happen unless the individuals involved have the capacity and possess the ability to collaborate. Each person must ask:

— Am I personally at a point where I have
   the capacity to be collaborative?

Further, the group must seek answers to the following questions:

— Do we have a spirituality which will nurture and maintain us in collaborative ministry?
— Do we have a process for moving in that direction?
— Do we have the skills necessary to be collaborative?

These questions will be developed in the following chapters.

"We Will"

Responding to the challenge and invitation of collaboration requires viewing a familiar picture through a different lens. The final decision, "We will," calls for reassessment, adaptation and re-education. The observations, questions, guidelines and challenges in this book are offered to stimulate ministers and ministry groups to discover methods of implementing collaborative ministry in their particular circumstances.

Discussion/Reflection Questions

1. Do I believe that collaboration is a desired and essential goal in ministry today?
2. How are we—staff, faculty, team—challenging others to minister?
3. At what stage of collaboration are we? How do we intend to move to the next stage?
4. In what areas do we need assistance to help us build greater collaboration?

Two

Obstacles to Collaborative Ministry

Movement toward a more shared style of leadership necessitates change on the part of the people involved. While the purpose of ministry remains the same—the mission of Christ—the method for accomplishing this task today calls forth attitudes, behaviors and skills different from those needed in the past. Even when the concept of collaborative ministry is attractive and desirable, ministers may experience difficulty in developing a more collaborative style.

Most individuals who are confronted with change show a certain degree of resistance. This resistance interferes with movement toward a more shared concept of ministry. If the goal is greater collaboration, then time must be spent identifying what stands in the way.

The following list represents some general obstacles. We suggest that readers identify additional difficulties based on their experiences. We also recommend that groups attempting to be more collaborative discuss how these obstacles may be present in their situations. The reflection questions at the end of the chapter can also assist in group discussion.

Obstacles to Collaborative Ministry	
Attitudes —competitiveness —parochialism —arrogance —burnout	**Behaviors** —hostility —unwillingness to deal with conflict —unwillingness to deal with loss —learned helplessness —failure to share faith —lack of commitment or training —failure to integrate sexuality

Attitudes

Competitiveness

We live in a world that fosters, values and rewards competitiveness. A spirit of competition can stimulate a person to explore new expressions of creativity and to unfold new avenues of growth and human potential. Competition among teams, for example, also illustrates the necessity for working together with others, for combining talents and gifts most effectively in reaching a goal. However, some people develop a destructive competitiveness that blinds them to the gifts of others or interferes with their freedom to unite their gifts with others in ministry.

Values are formed primarily within the family and secondarily in the school. It is within the family system that most of the attitudes regarding cooperation, collaboration and competition are developed.

A problem arises when overly competitive individuals are asked to participate collaboratively as adult Christians in ministry. This over-competitive attitude is the antithesis of collaboration. To teach students to value that which is countercultural and to form Christian ministers capable of functioning collaboratively are challenges that face Christian educators.

In addition to formation that occurs in the school and family, personal needs may foster harmful competitiveness. People engage in competitive behavior as a way of maintaining or building self-esteem. When self-esteem becomes tied to success rather than to the effort to succeed, competitiveness is destructive. These people equate self-esteem with perfection: "I'm OK only when I am perfect." This attitude inevitably creates problems when they are forced to confront their humanness and lack of perfection. They must seek some way to compensate for the lowered self-esteem that results from their failure to be perfect.

The method of compensation can take different avenues of expression. For some, the stark realization that they will never be perfect can trigger depression; for others, cynicism. Some will compensate with the fight/flight reaction, either becoming exceedingly belligerent or giving up completely. Others will settle for survival: "I think I can hold on for another year." Their philosophy of life is no longer one of continued Christian growth and challenge, but one of stagnation.

One of the more destructive reactions to the failure to achieve perfection is to attempt to build self-esteem by pulling down others. We once heard a story about an egalitarian society in which certain persons were described as knockers. Any individual who began to stand out or rise above the others was immediately knocked down. Ministers whose self-esteem is based on a norm of perfection may become knockers, unconsciously rationalizing their behavior by thinking, "If I can't be perfect, at least I'm better than so-and-so."

Destructive competitiveness occurs among groups as well as among individuals. Competition among groups is most intense when members' self-esteem is based more on the qualities and accomplishments of the group than on the self. In religious congregations, for example, the unique spirit and charism which characterizes the congregation can subtly become the basis for comparison and rivalry with other congregations. Teaching communities can begin comparing themselves with other teaching communities and can convince themselves that they are the best educators in the diocese. This can result in a condescending, arrogant attitude toward the other congregations. Or, a congregation that chooses a specific apostolate, for example, a center for battered wives, can believe that their group is more relevant and important than the other congregations involved in more traditional ministries. We have observed communities which boast about how superior they are to other communities because they not only work with the poor, but also live among them. While at times competitiveness is subtle, it sometimes becomes quite blatant.

A similar attitude can develop on a parish or school level, when healthy pride in the institution degenerates into an attitude of "our parish/school is better than any other parish/school." Within the parish or school, petty squabbles may arise between organizations. Wherever an overly competitive attitude dominates, whether at the individual, parish, congregation or diocesan level, attempts at collaboration will be virtually impossible.

Parochialism

Parochialism is characterized by narrowness of thinking. It often leads to an attitude of exclusive concern for one group with a corresponding apathy toward anyone not of that group. Unfortunately, in many ministerial situations vision can become limited to "my parish," "our school or hospital," or "my diocese." Since the thrust of Christianity is evangelization, not maintenance, parochial vision is contrary to the goal of Christianity. The gifts and talents of individuals or groups are given by God for the building of the kingdom, both in their immediate sphere and in the wider church.

We recently listened to a pastor from the Philippines describing his parish and a neighboring parish. We were struck by the attitude of collaboration and cooperation that existed between this priest and the neighboring pastor. Perhaps we felt this way because their attitude is more rare than we wish to admit!

The pastor reported that the parish he served consisted of 60,000 Catholics. Our surprise at the size of the parish was clearly reflected in our faces. The pastor then described the neighboring parish—120,000 Catholics with just one priest, a pastor who was 73 years old! The pastor characterized both parishes as vital Christian communities. He attributed this to two areas: lay leadership and collaboration between the two parishes. As he spoke, it became clear that lay leadership had been fostered and was now responsible for almost all the ministry occurring within the parishes. Also, the two parishes worked together whenever a need was identified. For instance, if someone worked well with youth in one parish, that person organized the youth program for the area, regardless of parish boundaries. If someone had a gift for marriage-preparation programs, that person conducted the programs in both parishes.

While parochialism can be seen readily in a parish or diocese, it can also exist within religious congregations. As congregations experience a decrease in vocations, the continuance of institutional commitments can become a primary concern and preoccupation. Religious congregations are being challenged to respond to the mission and needs of the larger church rather than limiting their mission to maintaining community apostolates.

A destructive element that can co-exist with parochialism is the development of a closed system. A closed system is one in which all the energy within the system is directed toward maintaining the system. The focus of the system becomes progressively more narrow and narcissistic. In addition, an unwillingness to admit new members who will bring new life and creativity begins to develop. Any situation—ministerial, community, parish, institutional—that has developed into a closed system ceases to be life-giving for its members.

Arrogance

Collaboration is unlikely to occur if individuals approach one another from a stance of superiority. Arrogance blinds people to the gifts of others as it attempts to protect their own images and self-esteem. It is one of the most difficult obstacles for collaboration to overcome because it is often deeply ingrained and hidden.

Arrogance results from an attitude of superiority and affects all subsequent behavior and relationships. When people believe that they have all the answers, they see no reason to look for complementary talents and gifts in others. Arrogance, like competitiveness and parochialism, may also develop from the need to protect self-esteem. When a person feels inferior or insecure, even unconsciously, adopting an attitude which conveys the opposite, one of superiority, can serve as a defense. Regardless of cause, arrogance is destructive to collaboration.

Arrogance can affect anyone in ministry. People in positions of authority may perceive themselves as superior to those they lead. Presumably they have been elected or chosen because their leadership gifts and abilities have been recognized and called forth. It is important for leaders to remember that leadership gifts and abilities are not superior to other gifts, only different.

On the other hand, people who feel stereotyped or victimized by those in leadership may compensate by assuming a posture of arrogance, often becoming extremely aggressive and vocal in denigrating those in leadership. If only those in authority would only listen to them, they seem to say, everything would be perfect. They may perceive themselves as better qualified and more knowledgeable than the designated leadership.

Arrogance is difficult to eradicate because most people find it difficult to perceive in themselves—although they can readily recognize it in others. It is a pernicious obstacle. We have discovered in our workshops that skill training in becoming more collaborative will not result in much growth unless we intentionally focus also on helping people uncover their arrogant attitudes.

We have witnessed countless situations in which clergy and religious have conveyed an attitude of superiority and arrogance toward the laity by presuming that they had much to teach the laity with little to learn from them. In reaction to this attitude, we have begun to observe some laity who presume that they are better qualified for some ministries than the clergy and religious, simply because they are laity. Both cases exemplify an arrogance based on role rather than gift.

Since arrogance is usually difficult to perceive in ourselves, we need the feedback of others to assist us in coming to fuller self-knowledge. One test of a person's desire to achieve self-knowledge is the willingness to seek out honest feedback from others.

Burnout

The large number of journal articles on the topic of burnout would seem to indicate the widespread presence of this sometimes vague malady among the helping professions, including ministry. Burnout is an obstacle because those who experience it lack the energy and/or interest to engage in collaborative ministry.

A review of the types of persons who are vulnerable to burnout can aid in personal reflection. In a comprehensive and informative article on burnout among those in ministry, Jesuit psychiatrist James Gill identifies potential candidates for burnout as those who:

— work exclusively with distressed persons;
— work intensively with demanding people who feel entitled to assistance in solving their personal problems;
— are charged with the responsibility for too many individuals;
— feel strongly motivated to work with people but who are prevented from doing so by too many paperwork tasks;
— are perfectionists and thereby invite failure;
— cannot tolerate variety, novelty or diversion in their work life;
— lack criteria for measuring the success of their undertakings but who experience an intense need to know they are doing a good job.[1]

The movement from being a person who is energetic and enthusiastic to one who is tired and burned out does not occur in a single step. Burnout is a gradual, developmental process. We have identified four stages through which a person proceeds toward burnout.

The initial phase of burnout is marked by an almost excessive, exclusive commitment to work or ministry. The ac-

---

[1] James Gill, "Burnout: A Growing Threat in Ministry," *Human Development*, Vol. 1, No. 1, Summer 1980, pp. 21-27.

tual amount of work is not as much a factor as the attitudes and beliefs that drive the person:

— a good minister is one who has no needs;

— a good minister is one who is always busy yet always available;

— a good minister is capable of being all things to all people at all times;

— a good minister knows that idle hands are the devil's workshop;

— a good minister has no time for or interest in developing any relationships. Ministry alone is enough to sustain a good minister.

Internalizing such a set of beliefs creates unrealistic expectations that lead to an absorption with ministry to the exclusion of other aspects of life. An inability to set limits usually follows. Little or no time is allowed for recreation, friendships or leisure activities. In short, those in the first stage of burnout become one-dimensional people who are obsessively committed to their ministry and who frequently convey a sense of pervasive sadness to those around them.

Persons in the second stage of burnout appear to be constantly tired and speak enthusiastically about how tired they feel. For them, effectiveness in ministry is measured by how tired they feel. In this stage individuals begin to question many of the values that have sustained them throughout life and ministry:

— What am I doing with my life?

— What difference am I making anyway?

— Is it really worth all the effort?

These and similar questions prepare the person for stage three.

The effect of these first two stages of burnout on collaboration is apparent. The invitation to minister with someone whose life conveys sadness and exhaustion is hardly attractive to healthy individuals. Such people tend to repel potential ministers rather than attract them. In addition, those experiencing constant exhaustion lack the energy to engage in anything beyond normal individual activities.

Burnout is actually depression, and in the third stage, in which a person withdraws from others and displays disappointment in self and ministry, this becomes more evident. Those experiencing the first two phases of burnout can reverse the downward spiral, usually with the support and challenge of friends or peers. However, in the third stage they avoid others and are no longer visible at community, parish or staff functions. Burnout victims may project their self-disappointment onto others, making them overly judgmental of situations and persons. This behavior tends to drive others away, thus creating further isolation. In addition, other signs of depression may appear: changes in sleeping and eating patterns, constant irritability, lack of enthusiasm or energy.

The fourth stage of burnout is characterized by terminal cynicism. Persons at this point experience an erosion of self-esteem. Frequently the lowered self-esteem is manifested as free-floating hostility; friends, co-workers and everyone around are treated as adversaries and are subject to constant condemnation. Persons in these last two stages often cannot accept support and encouragement from friends and may need the assistance of a professional therapist.

Terminally cynical, depressed individuals are incapable of collaborating with anyone.

Burnout results from a set of potentially debilitating beliefs and attitudes. The primary antidote for burnout is to explore those beliefs that affect behavior and seek help in changing those beliefs that are self-destructive.

In summary, the stages of burnout are:

STAGES	INDICATORS	BEHAVIORS
I. Obsessive, exclusive commitment to ministry	belief system that links work with personal worth	one-dimensional person, no interests outside of ministry, limited support systems, inability to set limits
II. Exhaustion and questioning	physical and psychological exhaustion combined with intense questioning of personal worth	constant tiredness; lack of enthusiasm; uncertainty about life's direction, personal worth and the value of ministry
III. Withdrawal and disappointment	withdrawal, disappointment with self and ministry, depression	avoidance of others, judgmental attitude, emotional and physical isolation, depression
IV. Terminal cynicism	cynicism, low self-esteem	free-floating hostility, "turned off" to everything, constantly condemning, energy focused on survival

Behaviors

Hostility

Before discussing hostility as an obstacle, it is important to make a distinction between anger and hostility. Anger, like any emotion, is neither good nor bad, neither positive nor negative. Feeling angry is not sinful, nor does it necessarily interfere with collaboration. Anger is simply a spontaneous reaction to some stimulus. Usually anger can be traced to one of three causes: frustration, a blow to self-esteem, or a perceived injustice. When one or more of these causes is experienced, a person feels angry. Anger, like all emotions, produces energy. This energy can be used to overcome the frustration, to build up the self-esteem or to overcome the injustice. In other words, it can be used constructively and creatively to build collaboration.

Where then is the problem? The problem lies in the fact that often feelings of anger are converted into hostility. While anger is an emotion, hostility moves beyond an emotion to become a behavior, a behavior that seeks out an object for the feeling and treats others as enemies. The presence of hostility poses one of the major barriers to developing collaboration. Where hostility exists, others are not perceived as potential allies but as adversaries to be overcome.

Unfortunately, anger is unacceptable and uncomfortable for many people, especially ministers. A study of priests in the United States identified the inability to be in touch with and accept their feelings and needs as one of the major problems of the clergy.[2] The study further stated that aggressive impulses, such as anger, were especially difficult for priests. In our experience, difficulty with anger is a problem for most people in ministry. When left unrecognized or denied, anger can be converted into hostility.

One specific area where we have observed hostility interfering with collaboration has been in interactions between male clergy and women religious. An article in *Newsweek* commented on the fact that these two groups exist to preach a message of Christian love but observed that "the challenge

---

[2] National Opinion Research Center, *The Catholic Priest in the United States: Sociological Investigations* (Washington, D.C.: United States Catholic Conference, 1972).

facing today's sisters and the male authorities in the church is to manifest that love for one another."[3]

Over the last few years we have observed a decrease in the degree of hostility between these two groups. This is due largely to efforts at increasing dialogue and understanding at many different levels in the church. One obvious example of this is the attempt at extended dialogue between the bishops and leaders of women religious on a regional basis.

One thing is certain: Anyone in ministry will at times experience frustration, blows to self-esteem and injustices. Feelings of anger are inevitable. The challenge is to discover avenues of expressing the anger constructively rather than converting it into hostility which ultimately destroys any collaborative efforts.

Unwillingness to Deal With Conflict

Acts 4:32 describes the early church as being of one mind and heart and sharing all things in common. But this description gives only one dimension of the early church. In other sections of the scriptures another dimension emerges. Numerous incidents of dissension and disagreement are recounted: The disciples argue over who is most important (Mk 9:3-34); Paul and certain members of the church of Jerusalem come into conflict over the Gentile question (Acts 15); Paul and Barnabas fight over whether to take Mark with them on their journey (Acts 15:36-39); Paul opposes Peter in public (Gal 2:11-14).

Looking at the total picture we see a divinely founded church whose members are very human and where conflict is inevitable. Suppressing conflict in any group results in apathy and tension which preclude collaboration. If collaboration is to occur, conflict must be confronted and dealt with. Too many ministers are so fearful of conflict that they constantly function from a stance of "peace at any price," not

---

[3] K. L. Woodward, "Vows of Defiance," *Newsweek*, March 19, 1984.

realizing that the price is a steep one. Failure to deal with conflict condemns people to a state of no collaboration.

For now, we are simply indicating that both attitude and lack of skill can interfere with the goal of collaboration. In a later chapter we will discuss the skills needed to deal effectively with conflict.

Unwillingness to Deal With Loss

The impact of loss on both individuals and groups has come into more prominence in recent years. Previously, when a person experienced loss or separation, the common advice that was given was to try to spiritualize the experience. Increased awareness that this approach might be harmful to individual development has led to a stress on integrating these experiences in a more conscious way.

Loss and separation are as inevitable in the Christian community as conflict. The pain and hurt, if unrecognized, can also have detrimental effects on ministry. Experiences of loss are one of the greatest causes of stress in life, and too much stress interferes with people's freedom to be with and for others. Again, as was true for anger, it is not the loss itself that is the problem; the problem is the unwillingness to deal with it.

Any loss is experienced on two levels, real and symbolic. The feelings caused by separation are not only painful in themselves, but they also trigger memories and feelings of previous experiences of deep loss. Since the psyche seems incapable of ever completely dealing with the trauma and grieving involved in the most significant personal losses, it stores part of that unfinished pain. A loss in the present acts as a catalyst to release the unfinished business from the past. This means that people are usually dealing with the feelings of many losses at once, one conscious and many more unconscious. Understanding this helps to explain why seemingly insignificant losses can often arouse such strong emotions.

Many conflicts that arise can also be attributed to feelings of loss. The behavior of a parish council, for example, that spends endless hours in heated discussion over such issues as the removal of statues or the altar railing or the replacement of traditional hymnals can be explained by understanding the symbolic nature of loss. In some cases the current issue serves as a symbol for more significant losses such as the relocation of a favorite staff member or even the pervasive loss of the familiar church they knew before the Second Vatican Council. The more that a person's sense of identity is intrinsically linked with a particular group, organization, or parish, the more intense will be the feelings of loss if the continued existence of that group as he or she knows it is threatened.

When feelings of loss are denied or not dealt with, they interfere with the ability to minister collaboratively. Denying the feelings engendered by loss can produce an individual who avoids intimacy and maintains an aloofness from others. Compassion, which is the heart of ministry, cannot be expressed at a distance nor can collaboration occur in isolation.

Realizing that people in ministry generally experience a high rate of mobility, it should be apparent that greater attention needs to be paid to the experience of loss both for the one leaving and the ones left behind. Unless the feelings of loss are acknowledged and dealt with, the ability to re-invest in new relationships or situations will be greatly impeded. You can't say hello until you've learned to say goodbye.

Learning to deal with loss can assist in developing more collaborative relationships and ministries. These general suggestions may prove helpful:

1. allow yourself to get in touch with your feelings;
2. speak with others about your feelings (keeping in mind that others may discourage you from discussing your feelings because such discussions

may stir up their own unfinished business with losses they have experienced);

3. find a way to meaningfully ritualize the loss.

Learned Helplessness

Although the term *learned helplessness*[4] is normally used to describe an attitude of victims of physical abuse, the concept may be applied to an undesirable form of behavior that often stands in the way of moving toward greater collaboration.

Learned helplessness is an attitude toward life that constantly results in a feeling of being victimized. In studying the victims of physical abuse, researchers have discovered that these people believe, as a result of past experiences, that they have no control over their lives. They are firmly convinced that no matter what they do, it will not effect changes; therefore, they develop a general attitude of passivity and hopelessness. The attitude becomes so ingrained that even when a successful outcome is realized, they tend to dismiss the reality and continue believing that they are helpless. The reality is not as important as the perception of the reality, and the perception leads to passive, submissive behavior.

The theory has profound implications for people in ministry. Frequently we encounter people who have developed a basic attitude of learned helplessness, believing they have absolutely no control over any decisions regarding their lives and ministry. They believe that someone outside themselves, usually someone in authority, has all the power, and that it would be useless for them to attempt to change even a difficult or a destructive situation. They feel victimized and angry. However, they are usually the same people for whom anger is an unacceptable emotion, so they store it in a way

---

[4] Leonore Walker, *The Battered Woman* (New York: Harper & Row, 1979).

that leads to physical illness, depression or passive-aggressive behavior.

People who function from a stance of learned helplessness have often grown up or been formed in a system in which they have been the recipients of continual negative reinforcement. They enter adulthood with low self-image and minimum self-confidence. They have difficulty accepting and appreciating their own personal resources and gifts. As a result, collaboration is very difficult for them. Their attitude of absolute helplessness and hopelessness seriously impedes their ability to take initiative, and they do not see the value in working with others to try to better a situation. Their attitude has a paralyzing effect on them.

We see this attitude in men and women religious and diocesan priests who experience depression and disillusionment because they believe they are simply filling a slot in order to maintain an institutional commitment. They believe that a particular assignment from the community or diocese does not make the best use of their gifts, yet they fail to initiate any change. They believe any approach to the appropriate administration is a useless endeavor, and they justify their behavior by calling it obedience.

There are instances where individuals and groups are overcoming this tendency to learned helplessness. In one parish, for example, the parishioners were informed of the imminent transfer of their pastor. Instead of passively awaiting a new pastor, they requested a meeting with the bishop in order to indicate the type of pastor they believed would be best for the parish.

People who adopt a posture of learned helplessness need the assistance of others to help them take initiative and reassess their capacity to bring about change. Since learned helplessness is the result of negative reinforcement, it takes a great deal of positive reinforcement and support to bring about the desired change.

Failure to Share Faith

For us, it is inconceivable to expect collaborative ministry to occur when the individuals working together do not share faith. Nevertheless, from our experience, sharing faith seems to be more the exception than the rule among people in ministry. By sharing faith, we mean more than saying prayers together. We are referring to sharing those graced moments of experiencing God in a special way. It is sharing, for instance, the times when people have found God in each other or among the people with whom they are working. It is telling fellow ministers those experiences which have made a person most aware of the presence of God in his or her life.

There are many reasons for hesitancy to share faith. For many Christians, especially Catholics, their religious training did not foster this style of prayer, and an introduction of prayer that is both communal and personal, rather than private, will probably be met with fear and/or resistance. For others, shared prayer is scrupulously avoided because it demands a level of trust and intimacy that is too threatening.

The one thing that differentiates a ministry group from any other group is its common mission, the building of the kingdom. If the group is to work collaboratively to accomplish that mission, then the members need to pray together and share faith in order to discover how God is calling them communally. We have discovered that groups share faith easily when two conditions are present: a climate that assures safety in sharing, and an expectation that sharing will take place. Not everyone will have the same degree of comfort in this endeavor. Sensitivity and patience are necessary to develop the climate for faith sharing to occur. Chapter Four contains further discussion of shared spirituality as one element of collaborative spirituality.

Lack of Commitment or Training

When collaborative ministry is seen as a value, then explicit commitment to its development follows. The two major criteria for evaluating the level of commitment are money and time. A quick look at the checkbook and the date book can reveal the level of commitment.

If a group sees collaborative ministry as a value, it will be reflected in the budget. However, a cursory examination of the budgets of most church organizations and institutions indicates that little, if any, commitment has been made to collaboration.

Besides the financial aspect, commitment to collaboration demands time. With the pressing demands placed on people in ministry today, collaboration will not occur unless there is a conscious, explicit decision to take the time necessary to move in this direction. Many ministers consider time to develop collaboration a luxury rather than an essential.

In addition to a commitment to collaboration, ministers need training. In the past, and perhaps to a great extent even in the present, training for ministry was focused almost exclusively on providing competence in a specific ministry. Little if any attention was devoted to providing the attitudes and skills necessary for working collaboratively. As a result, most people in ministry have been formed with the attitudes and skills to function well independently, but they find a more mutual and shared approach to ministry difficult. Even those motivated to move in this direction discover that good will, without the necessary collaborative skills, results in a high degree of frustration.

Formation programs, whether for laity, seminarians or members of religious communities, would do well to evaluate how well they are preparing their candidates for collaborative ministry. Some of the necessary skills that we have identified, especially the skills of working with groups and dealing with conflict and confrontation, are discussed further in Chapters Six, Seven and Eight.

Failure to Integrate Sexuality

Ministering in today's church brings people together in

personal and intimate ways. This can be threatening for individuals who have difficulty recognizing or appreciating their sexuality. Inadequate sexual integration can prevent participation in and even be counterproductive to collaboration.

Sexuality is a gift; it should be acknowledged, appreciated and accepted as part of the total person. However, past attitudes toward sexuality led many people in ministry to repress or suppress this aspect of their being. The challenge presented to ministers today is to discover ways of integrating and expressing sexuality in a manner that fosters their ability to minister.

Two ways in which a lack of sexual integration may be expressed are fear and obsession. Some people become inordinately fearful of working with anyone toward whom they might have a sexual attraction. These people often spend an excessive amount of energy suppressing or repressing the normal feelings, thoughts and desires that emerge in the course of daily life—energy that could be channeled into ministerial activities. Beliefs and fears about sexuality render them incapable of the ordinary encounters, relationships and honest self-revealing dialogue with those with whom they minister, prerequisites for people working together in ministry.

Lack of sexual integration can also give rise to an obsession with the sexual feelings that may emerge during the course of building pastoral or ministerial relationships. Then energy becomes obsessively focused on self or on the relationship to the exclusion of ministry. Either of these extreme tendencies is destructive to collaboration.

The last few years have witnessed an increasing interest in the topic of sexuality among ministers. Perhaps this is directly related to the efforts being made toward more collaborative forms of ministry. As people work closely with others on a day-to-day basis, they may be forced to deal more directly with their sexual feelings. As collaborative ministry becomes more commonplace, the need for assistance and education in this area of personal growth will probably become even more apparent.

Harold Searles states that people working closely with others in a very personal, intense, helping relationship often discover themselves feeling sexually attracted toward, or falling in love with their clients. Citing a number of reasons for this behavior, he suggests that the sexual attraction or the falling in love is not the problem; what is potentially problematic is the denial of this reality.[5] All feelings are communicated, even unconscious ones. People working in close collaborative relationships should not be surprised to feel strong emotional attractions at times. If these feelings are not acknowledged and accepted and, when appropriate, even discussed together or with a third party, difficulties in ministry will ensue.

Given the fact that personal histories may make it difficult for some ministers to accept sexual attractions and feelings, we strongly recommend ongoing consultation and supervision for all people in ministry. This supervision/consultation helps in uncovering and working through some of the unconscious elements that interfere with the ability to be an effective minister.

We also recommend that those involved in collaborative ministry attend sexuality workshops to aid in the greater integration of this profound aspect of life. The best sexuality workshops for people in ministry are conducted by those who are comfortable with their own sexuality, have a thorough knowledge of the field, and possess a deep understanding and respect for the Christian attitudes toward sexuality. In conducting sexuality workshops, we have been impressed with the intense need and willingness on the part of so many ministers—women, men, lay, clergy and religious—to discuss this aspect of their lives honestly and openly.

---

[5] Harold Searles, *Collected Papers on Schizophrenia and Related Subjects* (New York: International Universities Press, 1965).

Discussion/Reflection Questions

1. Are there ways in which my need to maintain my sense of self-esteem interferes with my ability to be collaborative?

2. What do I see as a major obstacle to my becoming more collaborative?

3. Did any of the obstacles listed in the chapter trigger an emotional response in me? What areas do I need to investigate further?

4. Besides the obstacles listed here, are there additional obstacles to collaboration that I have seen in myself? What do I intend to do to overcome these obstacles?

5. Can I identify at least one major attitude and one behavior which I need to address in my life?

6. What skills or education do I need to be more effective in collaborative ministry?

Three

Readiness for Collaborative Ministry

Collaboration occurs as the result of a deliberate choice. This choice can be made effectively only by those who show a developmental readiness for collaboration. Specifically, the more fully developed a person is psycho-sexually, the greater is the person's capacity to minister collaboratively.

Everyone possesses the potential to become a complete, mature individual, the "generative person" defined by Erik Erikson.[1] God creates people with an innate orientation toward growth and, given normal conditions, individuals move in that direction. In Erikson's model the goal of nor-

---

[1] Erik Erikson, *Childhood and Society* (New York: W. W. Norton and Co., 1963).

mal human development is twofold: to become generative and to develop a sense of integrity. To become generative means to grow in the ability to care for others; to develop a sense of integrity means being at peace in the knowledge of one's self, accomplishments and limitations.

A generative adult ministers as a self-giving, other-centered person and can function either independently or collaboratively. The generative person trusts others enough to co-minister in gospel-oriented projects. He or she is willing to initiate new projects, risk new ideas or support the creative ventures of others even when criticism may be encountered. Generative people are comfortable with their own human limits and frailty. They are, in Henri Nouwen's words, "wounded healers"[2] who can allow others to see their woundedness and sinfulness because they believe they will be loved in spite of their limitations.

Those who attempt to function at the generative level before they have successfully completed the earlier stages lack spontaneity, joy and excitement in what they are doing. Their ministry is burdensome. They are not usually motivated by being and doing for others; rather, their ministry is almost exclusively self-fulfilling. These ministers are especially prone to burnout.

Individuals grow to the generative level of development when two elements are present: challenge and models. As Christians we need to challenge each other to grow. And we must allow others to challenge us. Models are also important. Those individuals whose lives reflect a continual pattern of growth, despite their own human shortcomings and struggles, can help others set realistic life goals. Unfortunately, the models offered to ministers often have been so unique and so gifted that attempting to imitate them is more likely to be frustrating than helpful.

---

[2] Henri Nouwen, *The Wounded Healer* (Garden City, New York: Doubleday, 1972).

Erikson's model is based upon the belief that people develop sequentially through stages as they mature, with each stage building on the previous ones:

1. Trust vs. Mistrust
2. Autonomy vs. Shame or Doubt
3. Initiative vs. Guilt
4. Industry vs. Inferiority
5. Identity vs. Identity Diffusion
6. Intimacy vs. Isolation

Only after successfully completing the tasks of these earlier stages can the person reach the stages of generativity and integrity. Failure to adequately resolve the tasks of any particular stage interferes with normal development and the issues of that stage arise again in later life.

What follows is a model for evaluating psycho-sexual development and, therefore, readiness for collaboration. As human beings we are not finished products; we are always in the process of becoming. Therefore, we can begin with the presupposition that there are some aspects in each of us that are less than fully developed. This is not a threat but rather an invitation to further growth.

We urge readers to focus on self-evaluation rather than assessment and judgment of others with whom they are engaged in ministry. Our goal is to help each reader assess his or her readiness and capacity for collaboration. We describe some behaviors that characterize development at the stages preceding generativity and integrity. We challenge each reader to seek a friend, counselor or spiritual director who can assist in this assessment.

Trust

Collaboration is based on the ability to relate to others,

and all relationships presuppose the capacity to trust. Trust requires an underlying belief that the other person is basically "for" you and does not intend harm. When the earliest experiences in life reinforce this belief, an individual develops a capacity for trust.

A trusting person has

— the ability to differentiate between those who can be trusted and those individuals, based on past experience, who cannot be trusted;

— a basic attitude that others intend good, not harm;

— the ability to enter relationships anticipating acceptance and trustworthiness rather than rejection.

Autonomy

A small child is completely dependent upon adults. As the child begins to experience a sense of self, he or she feels a need to express this new-found autonomy. The classic example is the small child who learns and almost obsessively repeats the word no.

Collaboration requires the ability to function both independently and cooperatively. Certain people in ministry have been rewarded for being dependent and submissive and sometimes have experienced subtle punishment for acting autonomously. This makes it difficult for them to grow to this stage and collaborate with others.

Autonomous adults are able to

— be self-governing;

— avoid being overly self-reliant or independent;

— listen to suggestions from others, especially those in authority, without automatically reacting negatively or defensively;

— appreciate their uniqueness;

— make decisions contrary to the rules even when there is the possibility of rejection;

— enjoy a sense of control in their lives because they are willing to make choices, even difficult ones.

Initiative

At this third stage the child develops the capacity to take the initiative and begins to assume personal responsibility for choices. At times, collaboration demands taking risks and attempting new things, in spite of possible failure. Ministers who have developed initiative are able to minister creatively and are willing to try new models of ministry.

People who have developed initiative

— accept life's setbacks without failure-producing paralysis;

— are able to begin and maintain projects;

— make innovative decisions about life and ministry;

— identify personal goals and live by them;

— take the initiative in changing difficult, painful situations;

— do not allow fear of criticism or condemnation (from themselves or from others) to prevent them from taking action.

Industry

By *industry* Erikson means the capacity to work cooperatively with others. This stage occurs developmentally when a child moves away from the exclusiveness of the home and plays with other children. Ideally the child becomes less self-centered and learns to "give and take." Even the child's vocabulary reflects this change, moving from an exclusive use of "I" to "we."

Collaboration ideally goes far beyond mere working together, but it is only when people reach this stage that there are the beginnings of collaboration.

Those with a capacity for industry

— work cooperatively at task-oriented activities;

— recognize the value of working cooperatively;

— enter into situations that require "give and take";

— identify and value specific areas of personal competence and achievement and have acquired some level of self-esteem;

— are free from over-competitiveness;

— are oriented toward the success of the group;

— are able to share on the level of ideas.

Identity

This is the developmental stage of the adolescent, the person in transition from childhood to adulthood. The primary task of this stage is to grapple with the sense of one's own identity. It is a movement back from the "we" to a new understanding of "I." Adolescence is a time of self-confrontation, of assessing personal strengths and weaknesses. There may be reluctance to accept fully this newly-discovered self. New emotions, physical changes and the realization of limitations and inadequacies create high anxiety, a characteristic of persons at this stage.

People who have successfully accomplished the tasks of this stage accept themselves as unique individuals with limited gifts and strengths. They can engage in projects without expending undue energy in preventing others from knowing "the real me." They do not fear that they will lose their self-identity in collaborating.

Ministers with a strong self-identity

— are aware of their positive and negative attributes and are comfortable with themselves;

— have realistic expectations of themselves and others;

— relate freely with others as equals;

— become comfortable with their sexuality;

— relate well with those in authority;

— make choices, even when others disapprove;

— are able to make work commitments;

— are less influenced by heroes, idols, organizations or communities;

— are more flexible in thinking and decision-making.

Intimacy

In this stage of development the young adult is ready to risk sharing his or her newly discovered sense of identity with another. Secure in some knowledge of self, a person is free to merge with others without fear of losing his or her identity in the process. How individuals resolve the tension between intimacy and isolation will have an impact on their effectiveness in ministry.

When an adequate degree of intimacy is not reached, people are limited simply to performing the task at hand. Resolving the tasks of this stage, however, brings the ability to form commitments, to live communally and to minister mutually. Intimacy allows people to move beyond simply performing tasks with others; it enables them to share themselves and their faith.

Those who have developed their capacity for intimacy are able to

— establish, build and maintain relationships (more than one);

— share on many levels, for example, work, faith, experiences, feelings;

— share their positive and negative aspects with others;

— relate comfortably to both sexes;

— feel love deeply and love deeply in return.

The following chart provides a quick overview of the stages preceding generativity and integrity:

STAGE	DEVELOPED	UNDEVELOPED
I. *Trust*— believes that others are favorably inclined	basic trust, but selective mistrust	trusts no one; trusts indiscriminately
II. *Autonomy*—is able to function as a separate person	independent; self-governing	conforming or compliant; excessively dependent or completely independent; obstinate, controlling, manipulative
III. *Initiative*— takes personal responsibility	begins and maintains projects; self-starter	fears failure (does nothing); never checks with authority
IV. *Industry*— works and plays cooperatively	task-oriented; cooperative	obsessive individualism
V. *Identity*—has a sense of self	self-assured; accurate self-perception; comfortable with self	fears loss of self; over-identifies with group; defensive, arrogant
VI. *Intimacy*—has the capacity to share self	shares life, ministry, prayer; close friendships	cold, reserved; fears sharing

Four

A Spirituality for Collaborative Ministry

Ministry is the embodiment and expression of spirituality. While an action may be good, it is not ministry unless it is rooted in the intention to continue Christ's mission. By baptism all Christians are called to holiness and to ministry, that is, to a spirituality which has two dimensions, a deepened relationship with God and an expression of that relationship in action.

Too many ministers, especially lay men and women, evaluate their spirituality by the spirituality of past generations of religious. This monastic, individual spirituality suited the lifestyle of religious communities of the times. However, the same spirituality which provided support and growth for the ministers of previous generations may not meet the needs of people in the collaborative lifestyle of today's ministers.

Congregations writing constitutions and documents today often articulate challenging, prophetic mission statements, yet copy verbatim the sections on spirituality from former documents. This usually proves extremely stressful and guilt-producing for those members who attempt to be responsive to the newly-defined mission and ministry demands while at the same time striving to be faithful to the spiritual practices and devotions of a different period.

In addition, popular writers on spirituality, who offer a great service to the church, seem to find it difficult to distance themselves from religious-congregation-based value systems regarding spirituality and to articulate a radically different spirituality for today's collaborative ministers.

In no way do we intend to minimize the spirituality of the past which has nurtured and enriched so many lives. We simply offer some observations and reflections based on what we have learned from other ministers about their growth as spiritual people.

In attempting to formulate what a spirituality for collaborative ministry might look like, we repeatedly posed to ourselves and to others such questions as: How can an individual today develop an internal friendship with God which compels him or her to express that relationship in ministry to others? What qualities are characteristic of a spirituality that develops a deeper relationship with God and energizes a person to manifest that relationship in service to and with others?

The responses we received to these questions indicate that certain elements of spirituality are integral in the transition from a traditional style of ministry to a more collaborative one. The collaborative minister needs a spirituality that:

1. integrates the total person;

2. nurtures through reflection;
3. contains a shared or communal dimension;
4. is balanced;
5. moves him or her to compassionate action.

The following discussion describes how these qualities are part of a developing understanding of spirituality for apostolic-collaborative ministry. It does not attempt to define a perfected vision of a theology or a spirituality for collaborative ministry.

A Spirituality That Integrates the Total Person

Spirituality is one dimension of the total person, and continuous growth in this area requires harmony or consistency with the changes and realities of other aspects of life. Culture, sexuality, physical health, age, personality, psychological development and other factors all influence spiritual development. The following issues often emerge as areas of special concern and difficulty for those in ministry: coping with failure, problems in psycho-sexual development, particular circumstances, and recognizing and accepting feelings.

Failure

Perfectionism is an obstacle not only to collaboration, but also to developing a balanced spirituality. When perfectionists become aware of their limitations, they may become critical or judgmental toward themselves, others and life in general. They find it extremely difficult to appreciate their own goodness and spirituality when they face the inevitable failures that are a part of collaborative ministry as well as all other areas of life. These are the people who find it too threatening to their self-esteem to risk sharing faith with others. They fear that in the process of sharing, the others will become aware of their lack of perfection.

One solution is to help people move from a spirituality of perfection to a spirituality of failure. They need to know that they are good, spiritual people even when they fail, that God can be found in failure perhaps more easily than in success. People who have been reared on the injunction to "be perfect as your heavenly Father is perfect" (Mt 5:48) usually find it difficult to integrate failure into their spirituality. These ministers need encouragement and affirmation to become more accepting of their own brokenness.

A number of years ago Jesuit psychiatrist James Gill, director of the Jesuit Educational Center for Human Development, offered the following advice for developing an effective formation program for ministers: "Develop a program where candidates feel free to fail." Emotional and spiritual growth take place when a person can fail without losing self-esteem. On the other hand, when a person is protected from failure and is formed in the belief that failure is intolerable, there is little preparation for integrating the failures in life and ministry into spirituality.

During a workshop we were conducting for social justice ministers, the participants were asked to chart their successes and failures in ministry. Those who were able to accept their perceived failures also recognized the acceptance of these failures as times of spiritual growth. Those who had difficulty accepting failure often became fixated in their spiritual development at these times.

Jesus is the model for all spirituality, yet his life was a series of apparent failures. St. Paul wrote about his own failures, how he often did the things which he did not want to do. His life demonstrates how willingness to constructively accept failure can lead to new depths of spirituality.

Failure is a reality of life, especially for those who risk trying new things. Coping constructively with failure creates a freedom that allows ministers to share with others, especially those with whom they minister.

Psycho-sexual Development

The second issue of special consideration is the need to integrate individual psycho-sexual development into spirituality. Increased understanding of human development has heightened general awareness and appreciation of the differences that occur in individuals at the various developmental periods in life. Ideally these developmentally related experiences are integrated into all aspects of a person's spiritual development.

For example, those in midlife often undergo a period of questioning, doubt, reassessment and choice. This dynamic affects the whole of life including their relationships with other persons and with God. When there is an awareness of this predictable dynamic, the experience is not so threatening, and individuals are better able to accept and to integrate the disquieting experience as part of normal growth. When the impact of this internal chaos on spiritual life is not recognized or accepted, however, internal turmoil can result.

It is helpful for persons experiencing midlife questioning to permit the questions to surface and be integrated; to grapple with the inevitable doubts; to investigate alternative options in terms of ministry, prayer and lifestyle; and, to move to a decision and to a commitment or recommitment. The need to move away from familiar prayer forms to different ones may surface. This is difficult to do because at midlife there is frequently a desire to retain the familiar which may provide security but not growth.

Similarly, as people in ministry approach retirement, they often face a period of questioning, usually of a more specific nature: Have I been a good Christian? Will God be pleased with what I have been and done? Could/Should I have done more? What if there is no God? Because these questions can be frightening, there is a tendency to avoid them. They need to be accepted and embraced as sent by God to give birth to a period of integrity, peace and contentment in prayer life. If these questions are not brought to prayer, they often remain on the periphery of consciousness, leaving the questioner with a constant sense of disquietude and a lack of peace.

Developmental stages are experienced differently by each person. Even so, prayerful, encouraging support from others is helpful. The major value of a communal, collaborative spirituality is that this support can be extended by others with whom one prays and ministers.

Life Circumstances

Life circumstances also influence spirituality. We once visited a holy priest shortly before he died. He had been a source of edification for us both while he was ministering in parishes and serving as a political figure at the national level. His ministry was clearly an expression of his deep, personal relationship with God. He possessed a spirituality which nurtured, sustained and directed him in all he did. In the final years of life he suffered greatly from cancer and required numerous hospitalizations and surgeries. During his last days in the hospital, he declared simply and peacefully that he had to find a new spirituality at this point in his life. That which had sustained and nourished him in the past was no longer adequate. He needed a spirituality suitable for his present situation of suffering, pain and readiness for death.

Like this priest, each person has to search for a spirituality which is appropriate for his or her specific situation.

Recognizing and Accepting Feelings

The recognition and integration of feelings and emotions is part of human development. Their acceptance and expression are avenues through which a person grows into maturity. Some people, however, limit the range of emotions they allow themselves in their relationship with God. They may permit themselves, for example, to express their affection, but fear may prevent them from recognizing and accepting their feelings of anger toward God.

Collaborative ministry brings people together in numerous ways and may trigger a variety of feelings and emotions. It is imperative that people in ministry become more comfortable with their emotions, bringing them into every aspect of their lives, including their spirituality. Inability to recognize and claim feelings will undoubtedly hamper people in ministering collaboratively and in their spiritual growth.

A Spirituality Nurtured Through Reflection

Friendship with God requires time alone to deepen and nurture the bond of love. The relationship cannot develop into fullness without a reflective spiritual life. Quiet moments of prayer and reflection allow us to touch the source of life within, to gain knowledge of ourselves as gifted persons and to ponder God's continuing call and our response. Yet many ministers voice a concern that their overly demanding ministerial lives cause their spiritual lives to suffer; they find little time to be reflective.

Since priests and religious usually were formed in a quiet atmosphere removed from the hustle and bustle of normal daily life, they may have difficulty learning to be reflective in the hectic ministerial setting. Most laity, on the other hand, have developed their spirituality in milieus similar to the ones in which they find themselves ministering. They have, therefore, often developed a greater capacity to reflect in the midst of constant activity. Our experience in conducting parish programs confirms this fact. For example, homemakers recount a normal day which starts with being awakened by an infant's cries and ends with collapsing into bed exhausted. These same individuals talk about a deep relationship with God which has been fostered by finding moments in the midst of their tasks to converse intimately with God.

In conducting workshops in parishes, we often ask participants where they pray. Common responses are: the bathroom, the bedroom, the automobile, the kitchen and nature. Unable to remove themselves, these people have developed the skill of reflecting in the midst of hectic situations. They could teach others how to do this.

Some time ago we met with a group in the home of one of the group members. Pictures of the seven children of this family, one of whom had died, hung on the wall. Three of the children have muscular dystrophy, which places great time and energy demands on the parents. During a session on gift discernment the group members told the mother of this family the gifts they saw in her. It became evident that she was a woman of deep faith who radiated this faith and peace to everyone she encountered. Later, as she spoke about her spirituality, she described using whatever moments she could "steal" in the course of her extremely demanding days to develop her relationship with God. She is a model for her Christian community as she integrates reflection into her pressured life.

Like this mother, we need to function on two levels at the same time—being completely present to what we are doing while also being aware of the presence of God.

A Spirituality That Contains a Shared or Communal Dimension

During a workshop on the topic of shared ministry, a sister commented that if religious were to develop an apostolic spirituality to sustain and nourish them in the midst of a hectic life, they must be willing to learn from the laity who have developed a rich spirituality without the luxury of the prolonged prayer and contemplation times afforded many priests and religious. Clergy and religious, on the other hand, can offer the fruits of a spirituality developed through more structured formation. Priests, religious and laity will come to a fuller and richer spirituality when they acknowledge their own gifts and the gifts of others. This, however, requires humility. Sometimes arrogance blinds people to seeing and learning from others and prevents further development in the spiritual life.

Collaboration in ministry demands collaboration in spirituality. No one group can assume the stance of "experts" while others remain "learners." There must be a willingness and an openness to listen and to learn from those in different lifestyles. If behavior is a way of evaluating beliefs and values, then one way of evaluating openness is to determine the extent to which we have allowed others, particularly those in different lifestyles, to influence our spirituality.

We saw this openness emerge at a workshop on lay ministries requested by a congregation of men religious and attended by the religious and parishioners and staff members of their parishes. The discussion which followed the presentation on spirituality was highly theoretical and intellectual. The reticence of the lay persons, who had been involved up to this point, was apparent. We asked the lay participants what they were feeling during the discussion. Almost universally they described themselves as "feeling stupid." We then asked the priests and religious present to be silent and to listen. For two and one-half hours the lay people recounted personal stories of faith and prayer which were profound and deeply moving. In evaluating the workshop the religious noted this session as the most valuable part of the program. These men had benefitted immensely by allowing themselves to learn from the laity about spirituality.

Not only must religious and priests be willing to listen

to the laity, but they must be willing to share faith experiences with those with whom they minister. Lay men and women comment that they feel deprived because clergy and members of religious congregations rarely share their faith with them. Parishioners complain that they wish the clergy in their homilies would share more of their own spirituality.

Some religious congregations are developing programs whereby those laity and diocesan clergy who minister in the congregation's apostolates are introduced to the spirituality of the congregation. An important part of such a program is the congregation's willingness to allow those who minister with them to influence the ongoing development of the congregation's spirituality and charism.

What has been said for religious congregations also applies to clergy. In conducting continuing-education programs for diocesan clergy, we frequently ask the participants to share faith experiences. Often priests indicate that they have not shared faith with one another. One priest commented, "In the 30 years since my ordination, not one priest has ever asked me to share faith with him." After the initial resistance to sharing, there is generally an excitement and desire to continue. We encourage priests to share those experiences from the pulpit and to develop structures which allow those assembled to join them in faith sharing.

In working with groups who have had some success in their collaborative efforts, we have noticed one consistent characteristic: the ability to share faith. To share faith with another means revealing who God is for the person, and how God's presence is affecting his or her life. Questions such as "When have you been most aware of the presence of God in your life?" or "How have you discovered God through one another?" can help a group to share at this level. If a group is to become a community of disciples then the necessity of this faith dimension seems evident. There have been numerous occasions when we have invited ministering groups to engage in faith sharing, and the impact has been profound. The participants said that the experience helped to strengthen or to build trust, intimacy, understanding, acceptance, respect and bonding. This type of communal prayer involves sharing at a personal level with community members or co-ministers; it means being vulnerable.

Creating a climate which helps to overcome fear and encourages sharing is essential. When people are able to share faith, they usually experience a corresponding ability to work more collaboratively with one another.

A Spirituality That Is Balanced

A recent study from the University of Notre Dame states that "Vatican II taught that the celebration of the liturgy is 'source and summit' of the Christian life, but it also recognizes that there is more to the life of the Church than liturgy."[1] While the celebration of the liturgy is normally the most important source of spiritual life, it is not the only means of measuring spiritual growth.

It is our observation that many Christians do indeed judge their spirituality by frequency of attendance at Mass. Establishing Mass attendance as the sole criterion for spirituality belittles the spiritual life of the many persons for whom daily or frequent Mass is not possible. Developing greater collaboration in ministry calls for a spirituality that does not overemphasize any one particular means, such as liturgy, to the exclusion of all others. Such a spirituality allows for the reality that God touches people's lives in strikingly different ways; we must acknowledge the mysterious workings of the Spirit.

---

[1] David Leege, Joseph Gremillion, "Of Piety and Planning: Liturgy, the Parishioners, and the Professionals," *Notre Dame Study of Catholic Parish Life* (Notre Dame, IN: University of Notre Dame, 1985).

A Spirituality Which Moves to Compassionate Action

The criterion we suggest for evaluating spirituality is the degree to which a person has developed the capacity for compassion.

Jesus is the exemplar of compassion. Throughout the gospels we see his compassionate response to everyone in need. It is Jesus who provides a challenge to all his followers when he commands: "Be compassionate as your heavenly Father is compassionate" (Lk 6:36). For a spirituality to be truly Christlike, it must be characterized by compassionate action.

James Fenhagen describes compassion as "love empowered by holiness." He shows clearly the relationship between compassion and holiness indicating that "compassion is in itself an expression of holiness" and, as he states at another point, "holiness is the fruit of compassion."[2]

Unlike sympathy or empathy, compassion requires an act of the will. Webster's Third New International Dictionary defines *compassion* as "a spiritual consciousness of personal tragedy of another and selfless tenderness directed toward it." Clearly, then, compassion requires the ability to move beyond feeling and thinking to action.

McNeill, Morrison and Nouwen indicate why this particular act of the will is difficult:

> It is important . . . to recognize that suffering is not something we desire or to which we are attracted. On the contrary, it is something we want to avoid at all costs. Therefore, compassion is not among our natural responses.[3]

---

[2] James C. Fenhagen, *Invitation to Holiness* (San Francisco: Harper & Row, 1985).

[3] Donald McNeill, Douglas Morrison, Henri Nouwen, *Compassion: A Reflection on the Christian Life* (Garden City, NY: Image Books, 1983), p. 4.

Compassion not only conveys an understanding of another's pain or suffering, but reaches out to alleviate that suffering. This type of response stems from an experience of God's love and from a decision to express that love in action. It is through compassionate action that ministry becomes the embodiment of spirituality.

It is interesting to note the frequency with which the word *compassion* is used today. Perhaps due in part to a highly technological, depersonalized society, compassion is emerging as a need in today's world. A need is something so vital that unless it is met to some degree a person becomes sick or dies emotionally, spiritually and sometimes physically. The world contains many people who are emotionally, spiritually or physically sick and dying because they do not experience compassion from others. Thousands of people experience great loneliness and need a compassionate response from members of the Christian community. Since ministry is the intentional response to a need, then a true spirituality expresses itself in compassionate responses to those in need.

"When have you felt ministered to?" is a question we frequently pose in parishes. The most common response is that a person feels ministered to when there has been compassion. One man shared his experience after the death of a child. While many friends offered advice, it was those whose verbal consolation expressed compassion who helped him the most. Their response conveyed to him their presence with him in suffering.

> What really counts is that in moments of pain and suffering someone stays with us. More important than any particular action or word of advice is the simple presence of someone who cares.[4]

Truly Christ-like compassion is not selective but universal in its expression. Jesus reached out to everyone. Our re-

---

[4] Ibid. p. 13.

sponse as Christians cannot be limited but should extend to anyone we encounter. The author of an article in the *Hindustan Times Sunday Magazine* interviewed beggars, outcasts in Indian society, asking them if they recalled any acts of human kindness. One beggar responded:

> In my eight years of begging, I can recall only one instance of real compassion. I was ill and sitting on a *patri* (a low wooden stool) outside the town hall. I hadn't eaten for several days. I sat crouched up in my *durry* (carpet), sobs of grief racking my body. A *sardar* (sikh) walked past me. He stopped and came back. He didn't say anything. He just led me to a tea shop, bought me some buns and tea. We sat together silently. Then he walked away into the night.

Clearly this modern version of the Good Samaritan parable provides a lesson in compassion. Each day presents the challenge to discover those who need our compassion—in the home, in the rectory, in the religious house, in the work place and neighborhood. Who are the "beggars" that we pass each day?

Discussion/Reflection Questions

1. What do I believe are the elements of a spirituality for collaborative ministry?
2. In examining my own spirituality, are there aspects that I need to reassess in light of current realities?
3. In what ways would I like to see my spirituality
   — integrate my total person;
   — be more reflective;
   — be more communal;
   — be more balanced;
   — be more compassionate?

Five

A Process to Facilitate Collaboration

After reflecting on personal development and spirituality, the next step is to develop a process which will facilitate collaborative ministry. The desire for greater collaboration in the church is commendable, but desire, in and of itself, is not enough to guarantee implementation; there must be a process which will transform that desire into reality.

How this process will be accomplished in any given situation will vary according to the specific composition, history and goals of the group. However, it is our belief that there are a few key elements which must be part of any process if it is to lead to greater collaboration. The elements are:

71

— a vision with concrete objectives;
— a method for identifying the gifts of the community members;
— clarity of roles.

While the presence of these elements greatly enhances the probability for success, their absence may well subject the group to constant frustration and fragmentation.

Vision

To paraphrase Proverbs 29:18: Where there is no vision, the people perish. Many good projects, whether at the diocesan, parish or community level, flounder or fail due to the absence of an articulated vision which clearly defines the direction for the group. It is vitally important that a vision be clear, mission-oriented and mutually agreed upon by those who will be affected by it.

Jesus had a clear vision of the mission for which he had come into the world. This vision, to bring all people to knowledge of and union with his Father, served as the criterion for all his activity. Like Jesus, all Christians—individuals and groups—must have a clear vision which guides all their actions and decisions.

The choice to work toward greater collaboration entails the articulation of goals. Unless these are explicitly stated, a group may engage in a great deal of activity which leads only to frustration.

Even when groups attempt to define their vision, they may mistakenly develop a statement which is focused only on collaboration among a small number of people, such as a staff. If a group's vision is too narcissistic, a relatively high degree of ennui and depression can result among the members. As a Christian community, the invitation is to move beyond a vision of mere intra-community concern to one which aspires to greater collaboration with the wider community. A parish team, for instance, needs to think beyond collaboration among its members and ask the more important question: How do we find additional ways to utilize the gifts of everyone in the parish, the 100 percent of the baptized who have been gifted and called for ministry? Vision statements are most life-giving when they are mission-oriented and offer a challenge to incorporate and to influence beyond the immediate group.

Besides setting a vision, an added dimension must be considered: Whose vision is it? Only persons who have the opportunity to participate in the formulation of the vision will be committed to it. Elite groups which frame a vision and then expect commitment from those who were excluded from the process should not be surprised when they experience frustration. If the goal is collaboration, then everyone who is potentially affected needs to be involved from the beginning.

Although this is an obvious principle, many examples to the contrary can be cited: the diocese which develops and disseminates a mission statement formulated by a small group of diocesan staff or a pastoral council; a staff which promulgates a parish vision statement developed exclusively by the staff; the religious congregation that designs mission plans for apostolates without consulting those who will be affected. Where there is no vision the people perish. Where the people affected by the vision are not involved in formulating it, the predicted outcome is apathy.

In order for an articulated, mutually owned vision to bear fruit, one final dimension is essential: There must be an explicit commitment to that vision. If the group has developed a vision to which it is truly committed, that vision will begin to influence all decisions about priorities, programs, budget and time. Vision statements that are articulated in the comfort and serenity of a quiet weekend at some isolated location can soon be forgotten as daily demands are placed upon the ministers when they return to their normal setting. The challenge of a vision statement is to bring it to fruition regardless of the effort that is demanded and the difficulties encountered.

Many groups have struggled to formulate a clear vision statement, have devised creative ways of communicating it, and yet have experienced frustration because no growth has resulted. Unless the direction provided by the vision is accompanied by concrete goals and steps to achieve them, little change will occur.

The importance of specific plans to achieve a goal was clearly illustrated in a parish where the pastoral minister, a brother, was informed by his community that his ministry to the sick and homebound of the parish was limited to a three-year commitment. The community also informed the parish that they had no one to send as a replacement after the three years. The parish staff recognized and articulated the need to identify lay leadership to continue this valuable and necessary ministry. At the year's end it was apparent to the staff that nothing had occurred to bring the parish closer to this goal. Specific objectives were then defined to move the vision toward reality. The immediate goal was to identify 10 parishioners who possessed the gifts to minister to the sick. During his second year, the brother would spend 50 percent of his time training these new ministers. The goal for the end of the second year was to identify at least two people who had the leadership qualities to run the program and to see that, during the brother's final year, these individuals received the training necessary to take over direction of the program.

Identifying the Gifts

There are various ways to identify the gifts of the community members. Among the models which have been used successfully by ministry groups certain common elements emerge:

— creating a climate in which people feel free to discern their gifts;

— developing a method for sharing and clarifying the individual gifts;

— examining ways these gifts can be used in ministry.

Certain conditions are necessary to create a climate in which people feel free to discern their gifts. First, adequate time must be allowed for private, prayerful reflection on one's own gifts and the gifts of others in the group. Any of the scriptural passages which refer to gifts may be helpful. Second, physical surroundings should be conducive to dialogue. Third, the participants should know one another well. When this third factor is absent, the entire process may be experienced as a game or a playful technique. Finally, an objective presentation can help set the tone and direction for the gift discernment. Such a presentation could discuss personal obstacles which make it difficult to identify gifts, aspects of giftedness, and some examples of the meaning of giftedness.

The models which produce the most desirable results are those in which each person shares the personal gifts he or she has identified. The others respond to the speaker by affirming and naming additional gifts they feel the person possesses. It is important to keep in mind that many ministers overemphasize their gifts of *doing* to the exclusion of their gifts of *being*. A balance of the two aspects is ideal.

While gift discernment is usually a very affirming experience for those who participate, affirmation is not the primary purpose. The goal is to discern a person's call to ministry based on his or her gifts and to determine how those gifts can be combined with others for effective ministry.

Ideally, after the initial gift discerning experience, the

participants gather again to choose an area of ministry based on their gifts and the perceived needs of their particular situation. They then explore together ways in which their individual gifts can unite in ministry.

Clarity of Roles

The final element in a process to facilitate collaboration is the clarification of roles. We propose that those attempting to clarify roles investigate four areas:

— the relationship between roles and gifts;

— the degree of exhaustion;

— the extent to which ministry is performed collaboratively;

— the continuation of ministries.

Relationship Between Roles and Gifts

Frequently roles are assigned on the basis of a particular state in life or a specific sex, for example, "Father (*because he is a priest*) will lead the prayers" or "Mrs. X (*because she is a woman*) will take the minutes." On the other hand, there may be such a reaction to this stereotyping that Father is *never* asked to lead the prayers or Mrs. X is *never* asked to serve as secretary. Neither role nor sex should be the criterion upon which ministries are chosen. The appropriate question asks: Who has the gifts to best perform this particular ministry?

Ministers are most effective when the role required of them is compatible with their natural and acquired gifts, talents and skills. While this may seem like an obvious statement, it is not always the criterion upon which ministries are assigned or chosen. All too frequently specific ministries are determined by tradition, random selection or rotation. A planning process which helps identify specific areas of ministerial need and assists individuals to select ministry based on their gifts and talents is far more desirable.

What we are describing is an ideal. We realize that some church structures deny certain roles on the basis of sex or vocational choice. This is a problem, but it is also a reality. While we empathize with those who feel anger as a result of this situation, we also caution against converting that anger into hostility which destroys further collaboration.

Degree of Exhaustion

In group training programs we ask student leaders to assess their level of tiredness after conducting a group session. A high level of physical and emotional exhaustion can indicate that the leader is assuming inordinate responsibility for the group, thereby minimizing the potential of the group. Ministers can easily succumb to this same tendency.

The desire to serve and to participate in the church's mission can become overshadowed by the human need for affirmation and self-esteem. Assuming sole and complete responsibility for a project not only unnecessarily drains a person's physical and emotional energy but also deprives others of the opportunity to bring their talents to a particular project.

A recent incident on a college campus exemplifies this attitude. While the students and faculty members looked on, the campus minister prepared the altar for the celebration, served as lector, led the singing and then distributed communion. Her behavior seemed in opposition to the college's goal of forming Christian leaders. We could not help but wonder to what extent her own needs were being met inordinately through her ministry.

Ministers who excel at doing for others often find it difficult to be on the receiving end of ministry. These are the people who are always complaining of being exhausted. They are only comfortable in the role of giver, and can not allow others in the community to use their gifts in ministering to them.

Ministering Collaboratively

A major role for anyone in ministry is helping individuals in the Christian community respond to their call to ministry. The transition from the traditional role of minister as doer to minister as enabler is not an easy one and may trigger feelings of ambivalence. The desire to move toward collaboration is often coupled with fear. Unless there is willingness on the part of ministers to acknowledge ambivalence and to identify the causes of resistance, any attempts at collaboration will probably be aborted.

Ministers who believe that everyone is called and gifted recognize the gifts of others and challenge them to join in some form of mutual ministry. One way to measure our disposition toward enablement is by examining our ministry experiences. Are there aspects of ministry in which we could involve others? The chart opposite deals with specific situations, but it can be used as a model for describing our present ministries and our attitude toward enabling others.

Continuation of Ministries

It is often valuable to reflect on previous ministry situations.

— How many ministries in which you have been engaged have you passed on to others?
— When you left your last ministry placement, did the work continue without you?
— Had you worked with and formed others in the local community to take responsibility for the continuation of the ministry?

The ultimate criterion for evaluating ministry is often what continued after the minister left!

Individual	Advisory	Assistance	Collaborative	Enabling
"I do"	"I do, they advise"	"I do, they help"	"We do"	"They do"
I teach a religion education class	I ask parents about religious needs of the children	I have an assistant in the classroom	Co-teacher and I teach class, review material and decide content	Co-teacher alone develops and instructs class
I facilitate meetings of divorced people	I gather groups of divorced to help me prepare program	I have a divorced person assist me in the group	We co-lead group, share responsibil-ities equally	Divorced people run a ministry for one another
I visit a sick parishioner	I gather some people who reflect on the needs of the sick	I ask a parishioner to go along on a home visit	Parishioner and I visit the sick and share reflections on the experience	Parish visitation ministry is administered by parishioners

Given that the number of members of religious congregations is decreasing, religious can no longer be assured that they will be replaced by members of their own community or other communities. One pastoral minister, a sister, shared with us that in the last two parishes she had included in her contract that she would not be replaced by another religious when she was transferred. In both cases she helped identify gifted people in the local community who could carry on her ministry and arranged for them to receive the necessary training.

Discussion/Reflection Questions

Vision

1. Do we have a clearly articulated vision which provides us with a sense of direction for planning and evaluation?
2. Has everyone who will be affected by the vision been included in the formulation of it?
3. How does the vision explicitly challenge us to even broader collaboration?
4. Do we allow time to build the attitudes and skills necessary to accomplish the vision?
5. How much of the budget is allocated for collaborative efforts and development?
6. How committed are we to continuing to build greater collaboration in spite of the difficulties, conflicts or pain encountered?

Identifying the Gifts

7. When and how do we discern gifts?
8. How much emphasis is placed on gifts of being rather than doing?
9. How is the gift discernment process used to determine ministries?

Clarity of Roles

10. To what extent are ministries assigned on the basis of perceived giftedness?
11. Can I name the people I have challenged and enabled to become involved in ministry?
12. How would I like to change my approach to ministry?

Assessing Biases

Complete the following sentences. List the first thought

that comes to mind. Be honest and avoid any immediate censuring.

Most priests . . .

Laity . . .

Deacons usually . . .

Brothers never . . .

Sisters always . . .

13. Is there anything in the attitudes revealed by your responses which could make it difficult for you to work with some members of the Christian community?

14. Were some of your responses influenced by painful past experiences? (Realizing that isolated incidents may be continuing to influence present perceptions is the first step in overcoming stereotypes which may interfere with collaboration.)

Six

Group Leadership

Unless ministers have a degree of competency in the skills demanded by a more relational form of ministry, even the best designed process will not enable collaboration. We believe that the ability to work effectively with groups is the most important of all the skills required for collaborative ministry. Unfortunately, many people, including some ministers, presume that ministers possess the skill of working with groups even without formal training. Since this skill is essential to develop greater collaboration, formal training in working with groups should be included in ministry formation programs.[1] From our own involvement in conducting group training programs, we realize that the written word

---

[1] For more information about the dynamics and stages of community growth, see Rosine Hammett and Loughlan Sofield, *Inside Christian Communities* (New York: LeJacq, 1981).

cannot substitute for the variety of skills a person can receive in a formal training program. However, the following basic information can lay the groundwork for developing greater skill in group leadership.

A Basic Model for Group Leadership

The "rolodex method" for group leadership derives its name from the device which sits on many office desks. A rolodex serves as a quick reference for locating important data such as telephone numbers or addresses. The device consists of a series of file cards of information placed on a rotating shaft. A particular address, for example, is quickly located by merely rotating the files to the desired card. Mentally picture a rolodex containing just six cards with each card listing one function for the group leader.

1. to create a climate of safety;
2. to encourage interaction among the members;
3. to adhere to the task established by the group;
4. to direct the group toward the purpose;
5. to intervene when the dynamics prevent group progress;
6. to evaluate the progress of the group.

The leader follows the cards sequentially and focuses on one card at a time. When the leader is satisfied that the first function has been completed, the next card is flipped and attention is focused on that particular function. This rolodex method is a simple and easy way for group leaders to visualize their primary functions. When leading a group, some people have found it helpful to actually write the six functions on index cards which they place in front of them during the group sessions.

Creating a Safe Climate

Until there is a feeling of safety, it is impossible for the members of a group to apply themselves to their task. Since groups are by nature anxiety-producing, participants' energy easily becomes diverted to self-protection. Membership in any group often confronts a person with numerous uncertainties and insecurities:

— How will these people treat me?
— Will I be accepted?
— How will I be challenged to change in this group?
— Will this group threaten my self-esteem?

There is usually a greater sense of control in one-to-one situations than in group settings, and this feeling of less control can compound the anxiety level for some people.

The first function of the leader, therefore, is to create a climate in which everyone feels safe enough to share or to remain silent. If the climate is safe, the group can grow and achieve its purpose; if the climate is unsafe, the growth of the group and its members will be severely impeded.

There are a number of ways to build a climate of safety. The leader can put the group at ease by acknowledging the anxiety and asking what would help lessen it. Identifying and acknowledging the feeling as a universal experience reduces anxiety.

We discourage the round-robin approach in which the leader asks each person to respond in turn. The effect of this approach on some people is that anxiety increases, and they mentally busy themselves formulating an acceptable response. Since their attention is directed toward their own response, they are unable to listen to previous speakers. After speaking, they are often still not free to listen because they are now evaluating what they have said, deciding how it could have been said better, or assessing others' reaction to their words.

One way of creating a safe climate is to assist the group in clarifying its expectations. This is particularly important in the early stages of group life.

— What can be expected of this group?
— What is expected of each member?
— What can be realistically expected of the leader?

The time spent in clarification reduces ambiguity which is one of the primary causes of anxiety.

The leader needs to be sensitive, especially in the initial meetings, to anything within the group which may threaten a person's self-esteem. When certain threatening or aggressive behaviors are allowed to occur without any leader intervention, the members usually feel fearful and vulnerable. Scapegoating is one example of such behavior. One member or a small group of members is unilaterally blamed for any of the perceived problems in the group. Any type of behavior which puts down another, either directly or indirectly, can erode the level of safety. Most people experience a lessening of self-esteem when their person or their ideas are attacked. Others experience this when a suggestion or thought they offer to the group receives no response. Leaders who are sensitive to these destructive behaviors can be more assertive in intervening in ways that help everyone see what is happening. Of course the leader must be careful not to put people down in the process.

A further way of assuring safety is to encourage the group to develop an explicit contract regarding confidentiality. Most people hesitate to share in any setting where what they said for the group may be repeated to others outside the group. To assure confidentiality, the group members need to explicitly agree to certain conditions.

— Can the substance of this meeting be repeated to others?

— What, if anything, that is said within the group can be told outside the group?

— Are certain issues that the group discusses not to leave the group?

Problems regarding confidentiality are often problems of communication. Each person has a belief about what constitutes confidentiality. The internal belief has to be made explicit, and the group members must reach some agreement about their mutual expectations regarding confidentiality.

The leader should introduce the topic of confidentiality at the first meeting and again whenever new members are added. Once there is common agreement about expectations regarding confidentiality, everyone can be held accountable for honoring them. Anyone who believes that the agreement has been broken has the responsibility to bring this concern immediately to the group. A concern about a breach of confidentiality should take precedence over anything else on the agenda. Until confidence is restored, the group will not feel free to share on other topics.

Finally, leaders must learn to listen for symbolic language in groups. Group discussions which focus on people outside the group who cannot be trusted, for example, usually indicate that there is a feeling of distrust in the group itself. The alert leader can take this opportunity to check whether the feeling of distrust is felt toward the entire group or particular members.

Encouraging Interaction Within the Group

When the climate within the group is safe enough that the members feel free to participate, the leader can assess more closely the dynamics of the interaction taking place. It is in the early stages that a group tends to direct conversation toward the leader. The leader's task is to encourage dialogue among the group members. For some leaders this is not an easy task. Difficulty may stem from the leader's anxiety or need to be in constant control of the group or to be the perennial center of attention. Since the leader may be unaware of those needs and the resulting behavior, supervision and consultation may be necessary to help a leader recognize and change behavior which is group-destructive. Anyone who leads a group must be convinced that there is greater value in what the members share with each other than in what he or she says. Unless this is truly a conviction, no change will occur in leadership style.

As mentioned earlier, one way to assess the leader-centeredness of a group is to examine the leader's energy level. When the leader leaves a session exhausted, it is usually a clear indication that he or she has done the work of the group. It is imperative that leaders question their beliefs regarding the potential of the group and its individual members. Do they really believe that the group members have the gifts among them to accomplish the tasks they have set for themselves? If yes, then do they allow the group to exercise its capability? When a group feels responsible for what has been accomplished, the group experiences its own potency. This enhances the self-esteem of the members and gives new vitality to the group.

Group-centeredness can be fostered in different ways. First, the leader's simple verbal encouragement to talk to one another can shift the focus of attention. For example, the leader can refrain from answering questions which are directly addressed to him or her. It is a temptation for leaders to presume that the group is most interested in their opinions. However, as we have discovered from experience, once a leader suggests that the group first share their responses to the question, the group rarely returns to ask the leader's opinion. This can be a humbling revelation for the leader, but it is a valuable lesson for working with groups.

Our final recommendation involves behavior which

might initially appear as the antithesis of good ministry. In a one-to-one ministry situation it is imperative to direct full attention to the other person. This can be communicated in many ways, but usually it means looking directly at the person and conveying complete interest in everything that is said. Leaders who assume this same stance in group situations discover that it is counterproductive. If the leader rivets attention on the person speaking, then that person, in turn, focuses on the leader to the exclusion of the rest of the group. If the leader develops the self-discipline to divert his or her gaze from the speaker, perhaps by looking around the group, the speaker generally addresses the group rather than just the leader. For those trained for one-to-one ministry this approach is uncomfortable. The transition to a group-centered approach takes much practice.

Adhering to the Task

Once the members of the group feel secure and are talking with one another, the next function on the rolodex is to examine what the group is discussing. During the initial meeting the group should develop a contract which addresses certain aspects:

— What is the purpose of the group?
— What is the task of the group?
— How frequently will the group meet?
— What is the length of time of the meetings?
— What are the expectations of the members and of the leader?
— What is the policy regarding confidentiality?
— What is the method for including new members?
— What expectations does the group have regarding absences?

The essential element of this verbal contract is the statement of what the group hopes to achieve—its purpose. The group's purpose provides the foundation for all other aspects of the contract. While *purpose* expresses what the group hopes to achieve together, *task* defines the way in which it will be done. For example, a particular staff might decide that its purpose is to develop a working relationship as staff which will assist each person to be more effective in the apostolate. The task might be to meet to share what each person is doing in ministry and to hear suggestions which might increase each member's effectiveness. Once the group has clearly defined its purpose and task, the role of the leader is simply to determine if the group is doing what it has agreed to do. Ordinarily, whenever the group discusses irrelevant topics, the leader challenges the group to return to its task.

During the course of a group, it sometimes becomes necessary to renegotiate the task. This can happen when the group realizes that there are other more important or pressing issues to be discussed. For example, a staff may realize that it is more important to discuss the group members' feelings of loss and anger over the pastor's upcoming transfer than the agreed-upon task. If the group consents to the change, then the leader has the responsibility to hold it accountable to the newly defined task. Later we will discuss the leader's function when the group is resistant to the task at hand.

Moving the Group Toward the Purpose

If the group members feel safe enough to talk with one another and are adhering to the task, the leader has been doing a good job. Some groups continue at the level of discussion, but accomplish nothing. At this point the leader flips to the fourth card and focuses on helping the group move toward its purpose. Most groups fail for two reasons: There is no clearly articulated purpose, or the purpose is neglected as an ongoing guide for evaluating the group's progress. This is true for any group whether organization, community, team, parish or diocese. Although the primary efforts of a group should be directed toward achieving its purpose, there is a tendency in most groups to divert energy into many extraneous issues. When a group reaches a level of productive discussion, the leader must challenge the group to take action which will move it toward the established purpose.

In the example given above, the purpose of the staff was to develop a working relationship which would assist each member to be more effective in the apostolate. Given this purpose, the leader needs to raise questions which encourage the group to make decisions about how the members will personally and collectively use what they discover in the discussions to improve their effectiveness in the apostolate.

At this point it is easy for the leader to become overly complacent. Satisfied that the group is talking and is at peace, the leader may neglect to notice if there is any commensurate action accompanying the talk.

Facilitating the Process

The term *process* simply refers to what is happening in a group. It is this dynamic which demands the greatest skill on the part of the leader. Things happen during the life of any group which draw away energy and attention from the task at hand and focus on something which has become more important to the group. The group members may show an emotional response, the cause of which is not clearly identifiable, which becomes the focal point for their energy. When this dynamic occurs, the group is unable to focus on the original task. Either directly or indirectly it focuses its attention and emotion on the new, often unconscious, issue.

The following story shows the dynamics that may arise in a group.

A social worker in a government agency presented a tape of a group of prospective adopting parents for review and supervision. The social worker's concern was his inability to keep the group focused on its task. The purpose of the group was to help prepare the couples to be better adopting parents, and the task was to discuss their feelings and concerns. However, the number of available babies was limited, and only a few of the couples would receive a child. In addition, it was the social worker who would ultimately determine which couples would be selected. Despite the social worker's attempts, the couples resisted discussing the articulated task. Instead, they spent the entire meeting talking about the local football team.

This story is an example of a group in flight. The process involved their fears about any self-disclosure which could ultimately affect the social worker's decision. The fear was so intense that the group's energy was diverted onto a much safer topic. Once the social worker identified for the group what was happening, the members were able to talk about these fears and the double bind in which they found themselves. Consequently, the contract was renegotiated and the group was then able to pursue a more realistic task.

Process usually refers to the feelings and/or fears of the group members. Anytime the process interferes with the progress of the group, the leader's function is to recognize the fact that something is happening and to encourage the group to deal with the process before returning to the task. Due to the presence of resistance, numerous leader interventions may be required to force the group to acknowledge and to deal with the process. Because dealing with an emotional process is usually terribly threatening to a group, the members may unconsciously collude in order to avoid accepting and facing the reality of the present situation.

Some leaders become so process-conscious that they focus exclusively on the process to the exclusion of the task. A general rule for leaders is to focus on the process only when it obstructs the task, and only for as long as is needed. The leader may not always be able to correctly identify the cause of the behavior, but a general comment to the members that something is interfering with their ability to function adequately is just as important and can help the group explore its resistance.

Often when a leader attempts to encourage the group to deal with the process, the members respond by uniting in a concerted effort to "kill the leader." This is a defensive behavior which protects the group when it feels threatened. It is important that leaders be strong enough to pursue the process despite the group's anger. Leaders who are fearful of anger, conflict and confrontation can easily align themselves with the group, and this behavior can condemn the group to failure.

Evaluating the Meeting

The final function of the leader is to help the group evaluate its progress. Though important, this function is often bypassed even by very good leaders, possibly because it poses a potential threat to the leader's self-esteem.

The preferable way to evaluate is with the group since the members are in the best position to determine the group's progress. This can be accomplished by regularly allotting time for "post-grouping." Post-grouping consists of reserving about 10 minutes at the end of the meeting for the group members to become detached from the content they were discussing and to focus on the process and progress that occurred. Since the post-grouping is not meant to evolve into another meeting, the leader should be careful to limit the time. A typical post-grouping session might pose any of the following questions:

— How safe did you feel at this meeting?
— Is there anything which would have made you feel even safer?
— Did anything occur during this session which either

contributed to or detracted from a climate of safety?

— What one thing was most helpful to you? (Be specific.)

— What would you like to have seen happen that did not?

— During this meeting did we talk about what we agreed to? Did it help us move closer to our purpose?

— Was there anything which occurred that you wanted to comment on but didn't? Would you be willing to make that comment now?

— What would you suggest for making our meetings better in the future?

Often during the post-grouping, members who have been extremely quiet during the session provide valuable insights on the dynamics of the meeting. It is also during this time that the leader may be able to uncover the reason why certain insights or reactions were not voiced and can encourage the members to take more initiative in the future. The use of the above or similar questions allows the members to evaluate and to assume more responsibility for the success of the meetings.

Some Hints on Leadership

While our major focus in this chapter has been on a theoretical model for group leadership, we would also like to offer some suggestions on leadership gleaned from our experience. These suggestions concentrate on the attitudes and behaviors of group leaders.

1. Examine your own beliefs. Do you believe that groups have as much potential for growth as for destruction?

Testing what you believe about groups in general is a good starting point. If your group or community experiences have not been positive, it is difficult to develop a positive attitude about the value of groups. The leader's attitude will be communicated to the group members and can affect their expectations. When the leader communicates a belief in the capacity of the group to do its work, it usually responds accordingly.

2. *Think group.* One way to do this is to imagine that you are looking at the group through trifocal glasses. The first lens focuses on what is happening to each individual. The second lens focuses on the dynamics which occur between individuals within the group (Does A respond every time B talks? Does C always agree or disagree with everything that D says? Does the entire group tend to overestimate whatever E says? Does it underestimate any contributions from F?) Through the third lens of the trifocals, the leader focuses on the group as a whole. For most ministers it is easy to view a group through the perspective of the first two lenses. It is the third lens which presents problems, especially for those who have been trained in a one-to-one counseling approach. A leader's ability to view the group as a whole does not usually come naturally, but requires training and practice. Learning to think of a group as an entity rather than a number of individual components can help explain some of the seemingly bizarre behavior which may occur. This perspective allows the leader to see beyond individuals and observe the behavior that is reflective of the group. The leader can ask questions such as:

— What is now the major theme of this group?
— How is the group permitting or encouraging what is happening?
— How is the behavior of one individual expressing a belief or attitude of the whole group?

A leader's ability to perceive through this third lens is normally acquired and sharpened as a result of training and ongoing supervision. This capacity to "think group" is a distinguishing characteristic of effective group leaders.

3. *Focus on both the content and the process.* Most ministers have been trained to concentrate on hearing what is being said and may miss the more important message that is being communicated indirectly in the process. Training helps a leader alternate between hearing the direct communication and what Virginia Satir calls the "metacommunication," the communication which is expressed indirectly through allusion, symbol or nonverbal behavior.[2] Preoccupation with the verbal message interferes with the ability to hear the process message.

4. *Prepare for group meetings.* A good leader prepares for a meeting by taking time to review what happened at the last meeting, reflect on what has happened in the interim which might affect the upcoming meeting, and anticipate what issues, conflicts or dynamics are likely to occur at the meeting. The success of the meeting is usually in direct proportion to the amount of time the leader has taken to prepare for it.

5. *Reflect on all meetings.* In addition to the postgrouping which was mentioned above, we recommend that leaders take time immediately after the conclusion of a meeting to reflect on what has just transpired. Given the complexity of groups, leaders can never be fully aware of everything that has happened during a meeting. By taking some emotional distance, a leader may better understand the dynamics that occurred during the meeting. These and similar questions can help in this reflection:

---

[2] Virginia Satir, *Conjoint Family Therapy* (Palo Alto: Science and Behavior Books, 1967).

— What was I feeling during the meeting and what might this indicate about the group theme?

— Was there any time when I was feeling particularly uncomfortable or fearful?

— What could I have done differently to make the meeting better?

— What would I do next time if the same thing occurred?

6. *Trust your feelings.* Among the group leaders that we have trained, many have been sensitive to the emotional tone during a given meeting. However, we find that people generally need encouragement to believe in their own powers of perception. Frequently during a meeting the leader will experience feelings that are indicative of the emotional climate which, though not yet verbalized, is operating within the group. Trusting those feelings and thinking about their cause can help a leader decide the best action to take with the group.

Leaders need to identify the source of their feelings. They may arise from causes unrelated to the group; for example, the leader may walk into the meeting feeling sad or angry because of a recent encounter. However, if the leader enters the group feeling cheerful and during the course of the meeting begins to feel a sense of sadness with no apparent cause for this shift in feeling, the group may be unconsciously conveying this feeling of sadness.

7. *Be direct and gentle.* We have become increasingly convinced that the combination of direct honesty and gentle compassion produces the best results in working with groups. Many ministers are more comfortable with gentleness than they are with directness. The best group leaders are those who are able to integrate both qualities into their style of leadership. Leadership behavior which is both direct

and gentle helps the members of the group feel safe and have confidence in the leader.

8. Clarify and summarize. One of the best group leaders we encountered was a man who possessed an almost uncanny ability to listen to a group tape for five minutes and accurately predict what would occur in the group for a series of sessions thereafter. One might expect that his leadership of a group would include many brilliant and insightful interventions. Instead, 90 percent of his interventions were clarifying comments and questions. Later he shared his belief that clarification produces the most therapeutic results.

We too have found that occasional short summaries of what has transpired are helpful to participants. Leaders are well-advised to emphasize clarifying and summarizing interventions and to avoid seemingly brilliant interventions which usually only impress the person making them and confuse the group members.

9. Rarely bring closure. There are times when it is appropriate and necessary to bring closure to discussions. Yet some ministers have a propensity to put closure on everything. In many church-affiliated groups it is often beneficial to have people leave the meetings with some unanswered questions. The absence of closure can force people to continue their reflection between meetings and can encourage them to expand their thinking. For instance, participants in a bible discussion group might benefit from leaving with questions about how to apply the material presented or the discussion to their daily lives.

10. Make group interventions. There are two basic approaches to group work: to focus on the individual in the group, or to focus on the group as a whole. We believe that groups are more effective when the leader addresses interventions toward the entire group rather than any individual. Most interventions which can be directed at an individual can be expanded to encompass the entire group. The following example illustrates a group intervention.

During a staff meeting, a staff member asked how to deal with a feeling of intense loneliness. The other staff members quickly and almost obsessively offered advice which was of a highly impersonal and somewhat condescending nature. After the advice-giving had continued for a while, the leader asked if the staff member who raised the question was the only one who had experienced loneliness since the responses had not indicated that it had ever been a problem for the others. Slowly the other members of the staff honestly and compassionately began sharing some of their own struggles with loneliness. The leader's group intervention had moved them from focusing on one person to seeing the issue of loneliness as a universal experience.

11. Avoid the role of teacher or preacher. We have identified three categories of professionals who seem to have the most difficulty adjusting to the role of group leader or facilitator: persons trained for individual counseling, teachers and preachers. The latter two groups have a tendency to always have an answer and/or solution for any problem or issue the group raises. Many teachers and preachers find it difficult to enable others and facilitate groups. Their style of leadership curtails the group from discovering solutions. As noted before, people trained as individual counselors often have difficulty in focusing on the group as a whole.

12. Develop a sense of timing. The concept of timing in working with groups is one of the most difficult areas for group workers to learn, and also for instructors to convey. It is common for those learning to work with groups to experience the frustration of leaving a meeting knowing that there were moments when an intervention should have been made. However, by the time they had worked through the mental gymnastics of deciding on the perfect intervention, the group had moved to a different level or topic, and the intervention was no longer appropriate or relevant. The secret is to realize when an intervention is needed, and to be willing to make an intervention which may be less than perfect or even completely off target. If the intervention is made in a way that encourages the participants to disagree and/or grapple with what is happening in the group, it will usually prove valuable. Again, by taking time after the meeting for reflection, the leader can often determine what would have been a more appropriate intervention and be better prepared when a similar situation occurs in the future. Perhaps more important than the "right" intervention is a sense of the opportune moment to intervene and the initiative to act.

13. Seek consultation or supervision. Ministry is perhaps the only helping profession which does not require continuing education, consultation or supervision. This is particularly dangerous for persons whose ministries focus primarily on individual or group counseling. Meeting regularly with a person or group who will evaluate and critique their work helps ministers be more effective and can reduce the possibility of their harming the people they are attempting to serve.

Seven

Conflict

Two skill areas that are especially difficult to develop are the abilities to deal with conflict and confrontation. Although ministers realize the importance of these skills in developing collaboration, many also acknowledge that they find both areas extremely threatening.

Role-playing is often the most successful approach to teaching these two skills. By enacting a typical situation in regard to conflict, for example, the participants can identify the cause of the conflict, observe the dynamics that transpired during the role-play, and make recommendations to reduce, manage or resolve the conflict. However, the medium of writing does not allow teaching through role-play, so we must settle for a less dynamic and effective way to communicate these skills. We will discuss conflict here and confrontation in Chapter Eight.

Beliefs About Conflict

Personal beliefs about conflict and its appropriateness in the life of a Christian or in the Christian community make conflict situations difficult for many in ministry. The following list of beliefs provides a way to explore these personal beliefs about conflict.

Conflict is inevitable in the Christian community. The humorous statement, "Wherever two or more are gathered in his name, there will be conflict," contains more truth than most would care to admit. Whenever two people come together with their unique histories, needs and values, there is likely to be a clash of ideas, wills and needs. Therefore, it is no surprise to discover conflict among good, Christian people. On the contrary, its absence should cause suspicion. When conflict does not emerge in a relationship or in a group, it may be repressed or suppressed.

Somewhere in history, a myth developed exempting religious people from the universal human phenomenon called conflict. While the existence of conflict among God-fearing people might scandalize some Christians, its presence indicates life and humanness in the church. In fact, conflict has always been present in the church. The gospels, for instance, show the apostles in conflict over who had the closest relationship with the Lord. Perhaps there would be greater willingness to accept the inevitability of conflict in the Christian community if it were seen as a normal rather than a deviant phenomenon.

Conflict is never easy. Although conflict is inevitable, it is not our intention to present an image of dealing with conflict which is unrealistic or "pollyanna-ish." Quite the contrary, conflict is usually difficult, often messy, and frequently painful. While reading about conflict will not remove the difficulty, messiness or pain, we believe that through increased understanding there will be a greater willingness to deal directly with inevitable conflicts and a better readiness to manage or resolve them.

There is a difference between conflict management and conflict resolution. Many people approach conflict with the desire to resolve it, remove it and reinstate harmony. To expect to achieve this goal in all circumstances is unrealistic. While conflict resolution is possible, conflict management is often more realistic. Managing conflict means being able to live and work together even though the source of conflict has not been eliminated. An example will help to clarify the distinction between management and resolution.

When a certain parish council addressed the issue of the presence of statues in the sanctuary, two "camps" formed. One group felt strongly that there were too many statues in the sanctuary and that their presence detracted from the celebration of the liturgy. The other group felt equally strongly that the statues should remain since they had been there for years and had been donated by the grandparents of the members of the group.

Given such a scenario, the chances are good that the final decision will not resolve the conflict to everyone's satisfaction. Many feelings will remain. As a Christian community, the parish council must decide how to deal with the resultant feelings in a way that attends to the pain and hurt while continuing to work together to further build the kingdom. In this instance the conflict has not been resolved but merely managed.

On the other hand, the same parish council may be planning a parish renewal. Two teams are being considered to conduct the program. A number of council meetings are dedicated to discussing the relative merits of the two groups. Some council members favor one group; other members feel strongly that the other group is more suitable for the parish at this time. Over the course of the meetings the whole parish council decides that while either team would be a good choice, the first team is preferred at this time. This is a case of conflict resolution.

While we have used the example of a parish council, the application is the same for two individuals, a community, or any other groups attempting to work collaboratively.

Conflict which is confronted and managed or resolved leads to group cohesion. There are two important points underlying this belief. First, conflict has been confronted and not avoided. Second, as a result of the encounter, something positive (conflict management or resolution) has happened. Only when these two conditions have been met can the group achieve cohesiveness. Until this occurs, the group is loosely-related individuals who lack any real binding relationships. There is no community and no collaboration.

For too many people the norm within the Christian community is peace at any price, regardless of what that price may be. Somewhere in the recesses of the individual and collective mind is a menacing superego which reiterates a dictum—good Christians never fight—that affects behavior. The result is an unspoken collusion to deny the existence of any conflict. When it becomes apparent that the conflict can no longer be denied, then all energy is diverted to avoid dealing with the conflict. We are convinced that collaboration is only possible when individuals have the courage to acknowledge, confront and deal directly with conflict.

Another dynamic that often operates in the Christian community is the withdrawal that occurs when it becomes evident that a conflict is not going to simply disappear. The natural tendency is to give up immediately when the pain and messiness of conflict become apparent. However, in order to create Christian community there must be a willingness for the sake of the gospel to step beyond this natural reaction and to continue dealing with the conflict until management or resolution occurs.

Following conflict through to a point of management or resolution gives a group a sense of potency. The members realize that they possess the ability to deal with conflict without destruction of themselves or others. Failure to work conflict through to this point produces the opposite experience. An intensely debilitating feeling of impotency results from the belief that the group is unable to ever deal effectively with conflict, and behavior then becomes controlled by this fantasy.

Conflict which is not managed leads to pain for the individual and death to any collaborative efforts. Dealing with conflict leads to potency; failure to do so results in apathy and tension which are obstacles to collaboration. While collaboration is the desire to join others in uniting gifts for the sake of the mission, apathy is the antithesis of collaboration.

Conflict inevitably produces tension. People who work and minister together, yet choose not to acknowledge and handle the conflicts that arise, will create a tension-filled climate that prevents collaboration.

Approaching Conflict

Every conflict involves people who bring different personal histories and relationships to the situation. Each person has been raised and formed in a unique family situation within a particular culture and subculture, and these factors influence his or her needs, expectations, attitudes, convictions and behaviors. In addition, people sometimes bring to a conflict a history with the others involved in the conflict. Therefore, approaching conflict requires considering the individuals involved, the specific situation, and the relationships which exist among those involved in the conflict. Given that diversity, the following suggestions can provide a general framework for dealing more effectively with conflict.

Preparation for Conflict

Conflict would be more manageable if we knew in advance when and how it would occur. In reality, conflict usually emerges when it is least expected and often in ways never dreamed of. Since conflict generally takes people by surprise, those brilliant dialogues and rebuttals which most people have rehearsed in the privacy of their thoughts usually prove useless. When conflict erupts, the person's automatic response is to preserve his or her sense of self-esteem. This triggers a defensive reaction which interferes with the ability to listen clearly, think logically and act compassionately, all of which are prerequisites for effective conflict management. Instead, with the onset of conflict an unconscious or preconscious alarm system is tripped which sends out a single message: Protect yourself! The usual tendency is to defend by immediately attacking the other person. The more threatening the initial attack, the more intense the reaction against it. The conflict can escalate to the point where a rational solution is very difficult.

Conflict that can be anticipated is somewhat easier to deal with. Calling to mind a few basic principles can help in developing a more productive approach to the impending conflict.

1. Spend time clarifying the beliefs and attitudes which make you vulnerable to an attack.
2. Think about the needs, desires and wants of the other person (group) which might precipitate or escalate the conflict.
3. Consider the practical factors—timing, communication, knowledge of the agenda—which could negatively or positively affect the situation.
4. If possible, find someone to talk to in order to gain greater insight into yourself and your strategies for dealing with the potential conflict.

Ask yourself questions, such as those which follow, to help clarify your beliefs or attitudes about conflict.

1. What is my greatest fear about this potential conflict?

2. What is the worst thing that could happen if conflict were to occur?

3. Why am I feeling so intense about this? What are my needs in this situation?

4. What history about myself or this relationship is unduly influencing me?

5. What might be encouraging me to avoid or escalate this conflict?

6. What will be my first reaction when the conflict occurs?

7. How are past experiences with this person (these people) influencing me?

8. Have I stored up unfinished business that is confusing the present issue?

9. How does my stereotyping of others influence my perception of the conflict and the possible outcome?

Although the answers to some of these questions reside in the unconscious, discussing them with someone who will do more than merely sympathize can be helpful. The person ought to know you well enough to challenge you regarding your planned responses and the corresponding actions.

After reflecting on yourself and your reactions, consider the others who may be involved in the conflict:

1. What do you know about the others that might help you to understand them better and to react more compassionately?

2. What do you know of the recent past of the others which might influence their reaction?

3. What do you see as the strengths and good points of the others?

4. Do you believe that the others are basically good?

Again, it is important to go through this process with someone who will challenge your perceptions and prevent you from stereotyping others. The goal is not to label others but to become more free in responding with compassion, understanding and rationality.

Dealing With Conflict

Although preparation for conflict is important, it does not guarantee success. The following suggestions are offered for dealing with conflict once it emerges:

1. Acknowledge the presence of the conflict.
2. Define the cause.
3. Make decisions.
4. Defuse the emotion.

Acknowledge the Presence of the Conflict

The spontaneous reaction to conflict for many ministers is denial. However, attempting to avoid its existence usually leads to an escalation of the conflict.

We were invited to work with a parish which the staff perceived as "the perfect parish." The "perfection" was achieved by eliminating anyone who might potentially cause conflict, especially those who were most traditional or most progressive. During our days with them, the disenchanted members of the congregation became more vocal. In representing their discontent to the parish staff, we experienced a hostile apathy, probably similar to what the confrontational members of the parish had received. It became evident that the primary goal of this staff was to ignore the presence of

conflict. Since the ideas of the majority were never challenged, the parish continued to become more narrow in its
perspective, less creative and less life-giving. Only when conflict is acknowledged can it lead to growth for the individuals or group involved in the conflict.

Define the Cause of the Conflict

Energy can be needlessly expended in dealing with the
wrong issue. No resolution of conflict will occur until the
real issue has been identified and the energy has been directed toward it.

The most frequent causes of conflict are:

— threat to a basic need;

— poor communication;

— unfinished, unconscious personal development
issues;

— loss.

Needs. We believe that the most common cause of conflict is threat to a need. Since most behavior is need-directed,
discovering the cause of conflict begins by identifying the
needs which may be threatened. We will go one step further
and suggest that the most frequent cause of conflict is the
need to maintain a sense of self-esteem. Conflict usually occurs when more than one person's self-esteem is being threatened. Presuming that the need to maintain self-esteem is at
the root of conflict is a helpful starting point. In the role-
plays during training workshops, the place of self-esteem in
conflict becomes evident. When the participants are able to
dispassionately discuss the feelings they experienced during
the conflict, they almost invariably say that in some way
they felt their value as a person was threatened.

There is a direct relationship between self-esteem and
hostility. When self-esteem is low, hostility is high, and vice
versa. One person feels his or her self-esteem is threatened

and reacts by attacking others. The persons attacked experience a threat to their sense of well-being and counterattack in order to bolster their self-esteem. The energy of everyone involved is absorbed in behavior directed toward maintaining self-esteem. Interestingly, a sense of lowered self-esteem is rarely expressed directly but is frequently manifested in indirect ways.

The issue over which people are in conflict is generally only symbolic of a deeper issue which is unconscious and/or too threatening to express directly. This is especially true whenever an inordinate amount of energy is expended in conflict over inanimate objects. Notice the intensity of emotion which can be generated at meetings over such issues as statues, keys, cars, altar railings, song books, and especially the liturgy. An outsider attending one of these emotionally charged discussions would have difficulty understanding how mature people could become so distraught over seemingly insignificant issues. Since arguing over object-related issues is less threatening than the personal issues which they represent, group leaders must learn to think symbolically. When a leader can look past the intense emotion focused on some inanimate object and determine what it symbolically represents, the real issue is often related to self-esteem.

Personality differences, which are commonly labeled as the source of conflict, are rarely if ever its real cause. People are capable of working well with many differing personalities, and differences only become an issue when one person's self-esteem is threatened by the other.

Likewise, power is usually only a secondary issue with the primary one being self-esteem or loss. Power becomes an issue when people feel impotent. In such a situation, a leader can be most helpful by not directing a response to the issue of power but by assisting the persons in conflict to clarify for themselves the feeling of helplessness and its effect on self-esteem.

Poor communication. Conflicts which stem from poor

communication can be readily addressed and easily resolved. Unfortunately, any institutional system can be fertile soil for breeding rumors. For the person attempting to mediate conflict, it is good to ascertain the information base from which people are working: What have they heard? Where have they heard it? How accurate is the information?

Developmental issues. Still another cause of conflict might be described as unfinished personal development issues. No one has completely resolved all the residual conflicts from early childhood. Since the normal developmental tasks are not completed, each person unconsciously brings to new situations and relationships some of that unfinished conflict. One way people attempt to resolve the issues is by unconsciously projecting others into adversary roles with the hope that the previous conflict will be worked through in a more satisfactory way in the present. An awareness of this dynamic, which is called transference, can help leaders understand some of the more confusing aspects of conflict. By transference an individual projects onto others qualities and reactions that are more appropriate to people from his or her earlier life and treats persons in the present as though they were those significant others from childhood. Two important aspects of transference are: The response is usually more intense than seems called for by the present situation; and the present reaction is asexual, that is, it may be to a male, even though the original reaction was to a female. While transference can be positive or negative, we refer here to negative transference which causes conflict. Since transference is an unconscious phenomenon, a person's resistance to admitting it may be very strong. Outside of a therapy situation, transference is best dealt with in an indirect way that helps the person see others as they really are, not as the person needs to see them.

Loss. The final cause of conflict, loss, is often manifested symbolically. Loss is a common cause of conflict, especially in parishes. In the last couple of decades, many have experienced significant losses within the church. Where personal identity was intrinsically entwined with identity as a Catholic, particularly pre-Vatican II Catholicism, the loss has been intense. These persons may feel that they have not only lost the religion which had profound meaning for them, but also have experienced a loss of part of themselves. Loss usually produces great pain and anger. The anger can be suppressed, but it may seep out in conflicts over real but also symbolic losses in the present. This can explain the intense conflicts which emerge over such seemingly trivial losses as the removal of a statue or altar railing. Too often ministers attempt to address this problem of loss by offering explanations; however, the pain is not felt in the mind but in the emotions. If a leader realizes that the conflict is an expression of the grieving process and responds not to the object of conflict but to the emotional level of pain, then the conflict can be managed or resolved.

Make Decisions About the Conflict

Once the real cause of the conflict has been isolated, the next step is to decide whether it is necessary to address the conflict and, if so, how to go about it. Ideally those involved in the conflict should reflect on a series of questions which help produce clarity regarding the decisions:

- — Do we believe that the time and energy expended in working through the conflict are justified? (Some issues are so insignificant that they do not warrant the time that must be diverted from ministry to deal with them.)
- — How can we create a climate to most effectively deal with the conflict? (Again, when people feel safe there is a greater willingness to engage in conflict.)
- — Do we have the skills to work through the conflict?

(If not, the group should consider using the services of an outside facilitator.)

— What have we learned from past conflicts that can help with this one?

Reflecting on these questions helps prepare for the next step of dealing more directly with the conflict.

Defuse the Emotional Level

The suggestions for defusing the emotional level of conflict which follow are offered for every member of the group. At times of conflict group members can become overly dependent on the designated leader and can avoid taking personal responsibility for improving the situation. One of the major tasks at times of conflict is to defuse the emotional intensity of the situation to a level where people can interact rationally. When emotion is intense, most people experience anxiety which clouds perception and limits freedom to respond in a constructive way. In fact, unless there is a reduction in the level of emotional intensity, the conflict will continue to be fanned into conflagration that, like fire, has the potential to destroy everything in its path.

The first step is contrary to the natural fight/flight reaction to conflict and consists in remaining in the situation and attempting to become as emotionally detached as possible. While we realize this is extremely difficult to accomplish, we are convinced that it is absolutely essential in helping a group deal effectively with the conflict.

Like any skill, emotional detachment is not easily or immediately learned and is acquired only after many attempts and failures. Proficiency in this skill requires trial and error; those who quit after a single unsuccessful attempt will never acquire the skill.

Once some relative detachment has been achieved, the next step is to help others do the same. The goal is to move people from the heart where the emotion is felt, to the head where some clarity emerges, to the mouth where the people involved are able to dialogue. They need to discover they are allies, not adversaries. Obtaining emotional distance from the conflict can be accomplished by taking some time away from the meeting and suggesting a few questions for reflection and prayer. The questions should challenge the participants to think about themselves, the cause of the conflict, and some of the reasons for the intensity of their feelings. Since most people want to resolve the conflict, the time and distance will be appreciated, and it will be used to advantage. When the group reassembles, it is important to create a climate that facilitates the discussion.

At times of conflict leaders must assume a more directive approach. There are several things which can be done to help the group through this difficult process.

First, work at doing the unexpected. Since people generally expect others in a conflict situation to respond with elevated emotion, a response which is soft, unemotional and compassionate has a disarming effect. Compassion is the antidote for hostility and can frequently transform the climate and elicit compassionate responses from others.

While conflict emphasizes the differences that exist between people, the leader can help the group members discover what they hold in common. Individual differences are more acceptable and can be productive when the group members realize they share a common goal or belief. People are not always aware of their commonality, and once the areas of commonality are made explicit the probability of the conflict leading to growth is greatly enhanced.

During conflict the leader needs to draw upon the arsenal of leadership resources and skills that have been described earlier. The leader can:

— foster a climate where people feel heard and understood;

— challenge people to listen to each other;

— attempt to clear up any ambiguity;

— clarify the real issue and keep the energy focused on that issue;

— continually summarize to maintain clarity;

— explore the "why" behind the "what."

Although beginning counseling courses discourage asking "why" questions, we have discovered that most conflict focuses on an issue without any understanding of why that issue has meaning to the persons involved. When the whys are explored there is often greater understanding, acceptance and empathy.

Attempting Reconciliation

What happens after the conflict is just as important, if not more so, than the preparation or actual dealing with the conflict. As a Christian community we should not be surprised to find conflict, and we should be ready to challenge when there is no attempt at reconciliation.

Our recommendation is to attempt reconciliation, realizing it cannot be forced. Unfortunately, there are people who do not want to be reconciled and who prefer, for whatever reasons, to hold on to their hurts.

Many programs developed for priest support groups and for parish renewals emphasize reconciliation. It is the element of reconciliation which often provides the climate for real sharing and growth. Whenever there has been a rupture of relationships through conflict, we strongly recommend that there be some attempt at reconciliation. It is not the presence of conflict which impedes the continued growth toward collaboration, but the lack of forgiveness and reconciliation.

The following chart provides a summary of the stages of conflict discussed in this chapter.

Stages of Conflict

I. Prepare for the Conflict

    A. Clarify beliefs

    B. Think about the other person

    C. Consider practical factors

    D. Seek consultation

II. Deal With the Conflict

    A. Acknowledge the conflict

    B. Define the cause

        1. needs

        2. communication

        3. developmental issues

        4. loss

    C. Make decisions about the conflict

    D. Defuse the emotional level

III. Attempt Reconciliation

Eight

Confrontation

When workshop participants are asked what image they associate with confrontation, the responses are often described in negative, violent or destructive terms. Given these images, it is no wonder that confrontation is avoided whenever possible. There is a general inability for individuals to identify times when confrontation could be labelled successful. The general reluctance to attempt confrontation can stem from fears or negative attitudes and lack of skills which could facilitate confrontation. Like conflict, it is not confrontation which hinders collaboration. It is the unwillingness or inability of ministers to engage in confrontation when necessary which interferes with the development of greater collaboration.

One way to increase competency is to consider confrontation from the following perspectives: what, why, who, when and how.

117

What

What is confrontation? As defined in Webster's un-abridged dictionary, *to confront* means "to cause to meet," "to bring face to face." Though generally associated with op-position, confrontation does not necessarily imply that peo-ple face each other as adversaries; they can come together in friendship. For our purposes, to confront means to bring people face-to-face to look at the same situation.

To confront can also mean to place the truth, as one person sees it, in front of another. Since each person views life through a limited perspective, confrontation implies that no one has all the truth but only one aspect of it. An ex-panded notion of confrontation reduces the anxiety con-nected with it and affects why and how a person approaches confrontation.

Why

One reason for confrontation is to search for a more complete picture of the truth. In essence the person is saying, "Let me tell you how I see the situation. I realize that my perspective is limited, and I want to know how you see it so that together we can come to a fuller appreciation of the truth."

Confrontation generally accomplishes positive results when it is motivated by care and concern for the well-being of the other. A few years ago a member of a parish team in-dicated that she had experienced severe depression and burn-out. She shared how different members of the staff had con-fronted her about her behavior. The woman could only listen to those who communicated their concern for her; she "turned off" other staff members.

A pre-arranged agreement for mutual accountability can be another reason for confrontation. For instance, if a staff has agreed upon certain expectations, the members have a right to confront each other when someone fails to behave in ways consistent with those agreed-upon expectations.

Confrontation fails when the unspoken message is, "I'm telling you this because what you do annoys me, and I expect you to change." Usually the confronter merely becomes frustrated because the desired results are not forthcoming. Frustration produces anger which, in turn, will probably be communicated to the other person. This is far from the goal of confrontation which is to foster dialogue.

Who

It is evident that a person who confronts another should truly care for the person. When this concern is conveyed, a climate is created in which the individuals can dialogue.

In some instances, confrontation is delegated to a certain person because of his or her role. When a confrontation occurs because of role rather than concern, no positive results should be expected. In fact, when those in authority convey the impression that they are confronting only because it is expected in their position or role, the reaction is usually resistance or hostility.

When

Although no time is perfect, choosing a time with the greatest possibility of listening and openness on both sides is desirable. For example, confronting people who are physically or emotionally too exhausted to listen or share is counterproductive. Under such conditions, confrontations can easily deteriorate into emotional, hostile shouting matches.

Before initiating confrontation, assess the climate and sur-rounding conditions.

Both parties need time to internalize what is said and to engage in whatever dialogue is necessary to reach under-standing. The "Do-you-have-two-minutes, there-is-some-thing-I-want-to-tell-you" approach is generally doomed to failure. Absence of a sense of control often moves a confron-tation into a conflict. Informing the person that you would like to discuss an issue that will probably take "x" minutes, and setting a time to meet, gives the other person some con-trol.

Since the automatic response to a critical confrontation is defensiveness, it is advisable to tell the person what issue you want to discuss. This allows the other person time and distance to develop a response. When the dialogue immedi-ately follows the confrontation, the goal is often self-protec-tion rather than understanding. The initiator of a confronta-tion has had time to prepare, but the other person may be taken by surprise. Offering that person the opportunity to reflect, pray, or talk with another before responding to what has been shared often creates a climate for mutual under-standing and dialogue.

Finally, people operate on different time clocks. One person may want to resolve all issues immediately; another may need a longer time in order to dialogue rationally. This aspect has to be considered and discussed among the parties involved.

How

The skills involved in the "how" aspect of confrontation are the most critical of the five perspectives. The seven prin-ciples which follow are guidelines for developing skill in con-frontation. Some of the skills needed for confrontation are the same as those described in detail in the previous chapter.

1. When possible, confront in the first person. Phrases such as, "I heard that . . . " or "They said . . . " imply a "marshalling of the troops" and elicit a self-protective and defensive response from the person being confronted. Confrontations are usually more effective when the person confronting speaks about what he or she has observed.

2. Do not confront on behalf of others. An individual who confronts because of care and concern for the other person will be better received than an individual who confronts because he or she has been delegated by others. Sometimes a leader is asked to confront an individual on behalf of others. If a leader does not share the group's concern, he or she can be most helpful by encouraging them to do the confronting themselves. It is also helpful for the leader to work with the group to clarify the reasons and goals for the confrontation. Reviewing some general principles for confrontation is also useful.

3. Be direct and gentle. People who are very direct and honest, but lack gentleness or compassion, are often surprised when those they confront react defensively, aggressively or hostilely. Likewise, when fear of confrontation causes the confronter to be excessively vague in expressing his or her reasons for concern, the other person may leave confused, without even realizing that he or she has just been confronted. Being direct and gentle generally produces the best results. However, confrontation, like conflict, is never easy, and following all these recommendations will not assure success.

4. Keep confrontation in the present. A confrontation may move beyond present behavior to a litany of past behaviors. This kind of bombardment makes it impossible for the person to listen, and the purpose of the confrontation is undermined. When comments are limited to what has been observed most recently, the potential for being heard and understood is increased.

5. *Confront the behavior, not the person.* Distinguishing between the person and the behavior is not easy, and we merely suggest that working to develop this discriminating posture is a good principle. However, there is no assurance that the person being confronted will be able to make the same distinction.

6. *Never interpret behavior.* Confrontations can readily erupt into irreconcilable conflicts when confronters go beyond describing what they have observed and ascribe intentions to the behavior. "You did thus and so because. . . . " No one can interpret the causes of another's behavior based solely on observation. Any given behavior can have multiple causes. For example, a person's roommates may not have washed the dishes as they had agreed to do because they forgot; they were being hostile; they were called out on emergency; they are immature and irresponsible; they have an aversion to order; they see messy dishes as "homey."

The difficulty rests in the fact that we interpret another person's behavior in the light of our own personal experiences, history and beliefs. Each person's experiences help to form his or her beliefs. Beliefs produce feelings and needs which, in turn, are often expressed as behavior.

experience ➤ beliefs ➤ feelings ➤ behavior

An observer sees only the outcome of the process, not the steps leading up to it. For instance, suppose that whenever Mr. Z talks at a staff meeting, no one responds. Mr. Z may assume that everyone thinks what he says is stupid or of little importance. Actually, it may be that Mr. Z's comments are so profound that everyone else becomes reflective. However, Mr. Z may begin to feel stupid; his self-esteem is lowered. As a result he becomes very withdrawn and stops contributing at meetings. The only thing that the others see is his now silent behavior, and all sorts of incorrect interpretations could be ascribed to it.

Confrontation should be limited to observed behavior, the only area where there is any certainty, and no attempt should be made to analyze the causes of the behavior.

7. Be willing to listen and to be confronted by those whom you confront. This is perhaps the most frightening part of confrontation, as well as the most important. Beginning from the premises that each person has only a part of the truth and that one of the goals in confrontation is to come to a fuller appreciation of the truth, it is essential that the other be encouraged to share how the situation looks from his or her perspective. In the above example, suppose Mrs. Q became concerned about Mr. Z's silence and decided to confront him about it. Hopefully Mrs. Q would listen to Mr. Z describe the situation as he experienced it, and together they could dialogue in order to develop a fuller picture. Confrontation is most productive when all the parties involved are willing to be confronted with new pieces of the truth.

As a final point, there are times after confrontation has occurred when someone in authority has to intervene. For example, if an alcoholic person has been confronted about his or her self-destructive behavior and has not changed, then in charity and justice a person in authority may have to inform the alcoholic that a decision has been made, for example, that he or she will go to a treatment center. However, a decision should be imposed only after confrontation has been tried.

Nine

Collaboration in Practice

Translating the ideal into reality in our present ministry setting is a challenge. Obviously there is no one way or method of developing greater collaboration. Each situation is unique, and what is appropriate for one setting may not be beneficial in another. There are, however, four general principles which foster collaboration. We offer these for your consideration along with examples of these principles applied to specific instances.

— Dialogue is essential for collaboration.
— Collaboration is most effective when it is based on giftedness.
— Unnecessary duplication should be avoided.

— It is important to provide opportunities and structures for collaboration.

Dialogue

Dialogue is a prerequisite; without it collaboration is virtually impossible. In order for ministers to work effectively together there must be willingness as well as opportunities for honest, open and frequent dialogue.

- The Franciscan Sisters of Clinton, Iowa, expressed their belief that it would be inappropriate to engage in future ministry planning without involving the people who would be affected by their decisions. They invited all those working with them in ministry to attend a day of their chapter meeting. There were as many lay persons as sisters present for the discussion on future directions for ministry. The sisters spent the first day listening to the lay people and then dialoguing with them. As a result, the chapter decisions of the following day reflected the interchange and increased the possibility of more collaboration in the future.

- The Irish Province of the Society of Jesus assembled the faculty members of all the Jesuit colleges for the purpose of developing vision statements for their respective schools. Besides working together to create the vision statements, an important part of the week-long meeting was discussing the dynamics of the lay-religious dimension and how it facilitates or hinders collaborative educational efforts.

- Prior to a meeting of men and women ministers, there was some concern that there would be conflict between the two groups. As facilitators for the meeting we designed a process that allowed time for discussion in order to avoid any unnecessary conflict. The purpose of the group sharing was to increase appreciation and understanding of one another. After the participants dialogued as equals, expectations of conflict dissipated, and the meeting was characterized by a climate of honest and respectful discussion.

- In the Archdiocese of Chicago and the Diocese of Brooklyn, as well as in other areas of the country, grassroots gatherings are bringing together women religious and clergy for the purpose of building greater mutuality between the two groups through dialogue. As part of their meetings, the groups can discuss ideas for improving collaboration as well as past experiences that may have hindered their ability to collaborate. Although these types of gatherings demand willingness and commitment from the participants, they are positive steps in collaboration.

Giftedness

There should be a direct correlation between a person's gifts and his or her ministry. Collaborative ministry consists in discovering ways of uniting various gifts to accomplish the mission of the Lord. For this to occur, those who wish to minister collaboratively must have the opportunity to engage in mutual discernment of gifts. Those who do so tend to work together in a complementary rather than competitive fashion.

Parish staffs, faculties, teams and religious congregations that have used a gift-discernment model as part of their ongoing development have discovered that, in general, greater bonding, acceptance and collaboration resulted. Living and/or working together for prolonged periods can make people painfully aware of one another's faults and failings. Conscious attention to others' gifts creates an atmosphere of mutual respect and serves to enhance self-esteem, both important elements for mutuality in ministry.

- The vitality of parish life and the degree of collaboration among the parishioners of St. Mary's, Colt's Neck, New Jersey, is impressive. One apparent reason for this vitality is the unique way in which parishioners are helped to identify and develop their gifts. The experiences of personal tragedy and crisis—the death of a child, cancer, alcoholism—contain potential gifts which are frequently overlooked. This parish helps its people to identify the gifts received through tragedy. It then provides the personal support and training needed for the individual so that the gift can serve others. Finally, the individuals are listed in the parish directory as resources for those with similar tragedies.

- Our Lady of Divine Providence, New Orleans, Louisiana, has set the formation, training and development of the parishioners for ministry as a top priority in the budget. This parish does not hesitate to invest its money in providing the parishioners with opportunities to maximize their giftedness. For example, the parish decided to financially sponsor a trip to a national conference for all parishioners involved in the ministry of evangelization.

- In some countries, such as Ireland, the conference of major superiors of religious communities is composed of both men and women. A single organization offers not only a richness in diversity of gifts, in projects, discussions and so forth, but also serves as witness to the Christian community of the value of male and female collaboration.

- A regional meeting of the Leadership Conference of Women Religious in the United States chose collaboration as a topic. It was their hope to explore creative ways in which the unique charisms and gifts of the different religious congregations could better work together. While this was the initial intent, it became clear to the members that the approach was too limiting, and they should try to include the gifts of the wider Christian community. They expanded the discussion to consider ways of collaborating with the laity and the clergy as well.

- In a Florida parish a large number of the parishioners are home-bound. One staff member pointed out that in the concern to minister to the group, the gifts which the homebound could bring to the parish had been overlooked. A visitation of the home-bound population was undertaken, and the shut-ins were asked to identify their gifts. Two gifts emerged with great consistency: prayerfulness and time. As a result of the discernment, each home-bound parishioner was invited to become a minister of prayer for the parish. Those who agreed were formally installed as ministers of prayer during a service in their home. Each one was presented with a framed certificate along with a special prayer book and rosary. Each home-bound minister was visited weekly by another parishioner who brought the prayer petitions from the parish. The gifts of an entire segment of the parish which had been overlooked up to this point were now included in a meaningful way.

- A parish in Auburn, California, eschewed the usual method of nomination and election of the pastoral council. Instead, they first identified specific gifts that would be needed. Then, at the conclusion of a three-night parish renewal which included a gift-discernment process, those people who possessed the gifts needed for the pastoral council were chosen. The council has proven quite effective.

- The lay ministries program of the Diocese of Brownsville, Texas, is modeled on a concept of small learning-support groups. During the first year of the program, priests and religious were recruited as small-group leaders. By the third year of the program the situation had changed. Most of the small-group leaders were former lay participants of the program who had been identified as possessing gifts for leadership. The religious and clergy who also possessed those gifts were retained as small-group leaders. The ministry is now assigned on the basis of perceived giftedness rather than lifestyle or vocation.

- A number of dioceses and religious congregations are beginning to explore gift-discernment models as a means of assigning personnel. Such a model usually includes a method for assessing both needs and gifts. Since it is a radical way of assigning personnel, it is not being used with great regularity but hopefully will be employed more in the future. Gift discernment used in conjunction with a life-planning model can produce the best results for ministry placement.

Duplication

When institutions, dioceses or congregations think parochially there is a tendency toward costly duplication in terms of services, programs and utilization of outside resources. The following examples show what can happen when people start from a stance of working together.

- A deanery of inner-city pastors who were committed to becoming more collaborative invited us to consult with them and to facilitate a meeting to discuss some concrete plans for collaboration. In the course of the discussions, they arrived at three conclusions:
  1. There were too many parishes in the area. This resulted in many Sunday Masses which were poorly attended, and which did not provide quality liturgical experiences for the people.
  2. Evangelization was a priority. Each parish was currently developing and conducting its own evangelization program.
  3. The elementary schools were one of the primary ve-

hicles for evangelization. However, the 10 small parish schools, understaffed and poorly equipped, did not facilitate the quality education which was desired.

Further discussion led the pastors to the logical collaborative decisions:

1. to coordinate schedules among the parishes and to schedule fewer Sunday liturgies;

2. to investigate the possibility of conducting deanery rather than parish evangelization programs;

3. to recommend to the archbishop the closing of six schools and the merging of resources to establish four quality regional schools.

- Another example of this principle of non-duplication is an agreement among a number of religious congregations in one geographic locale. When one congregation secures an outside resource person, all the other congregations are contacted. The other congregations are free to participate in the program or to enlist the services of the resource person while he or she is in the area.

- The Archdiocese of New Orleans, which was contemplating the establishment of a diocesan lay ministry program, proceeded in a way contrary to the norm. Rather than immediately creating a new office for lay ministries, the diocesan agencies already involved in lay ministry training were convened. Representatives from the diaconate program, youth ministry, Catholic Charities, religious education, the seminary, the Office of Worship and Office of Family Life met to share current efforts in lay ministry. Over the course of a few months they were able to identify the courses and programs currently being offered, the resources available in the area, the ways in which they could concretely collaborate with one another, and the areas not adequately covered in the formation and training of ministry candidates in each of the existing programs.

As a result of their ongoing communication, the spiritual formation of the candidates was identified as an area that was missing from most of the formation programs. Instead of suggesting the establishment of a new office, the committee recommended that one of the existing offices be funded for an additional staff person. This staff member develops the methods for providing spiritual development for all the lay ministry candidates in the diocese and serves as a liaison among the existing agencies so that the process of collaboration will continue.

Opportunities and Structures for Collaboration

One of the major changes that has taken place in religious congregations since the Second Vatican Council has been the movement from self-contained communities to more open systems. Communities are working in conjunction with other communities at all levels, but perhaps collaboration is most evident in the areas of initial formation and vocational recruitment. Most urban areas have initiated inter-congregational novitiate programs that provide a milieu where men and women from different congregations can dialogue and study ministry and community life. Today it is rare for a seminary to serve only one congregation or one diocese. Collaboration in theological unions and coalitions is providing a greater quality of theological education for candidates.

- Inter-diocesan efforts, such as state Catholic conferences, have done much to combine and increase the resources of different dioceses as well as to influence legislation which fosters human development. In Louisiana, for example, diocesan directors from all the dioceses in the state convene regularly to share resources and information in such areas as education, social justice and so forth. In addition, the bishops, together with a group of representatives of the clergy from each diocese, explore ways of fostering greater collaboration within the state.

- The Missionary Servants of the Most Holy Trinity, along with a congregation of women religious, emerged from a lay apostolate group. The lay group, the two religious communities and a recently developed Pious Union function whenever possible as a family in the church to carry out their common mission. One of the reasons for their relative success has been the opportunities afforded them to maximize communication and collaboration. The general councils of each group meet regularly to plan and to evaluate. Members of the four groups offer retreats each year. Some of the initial formation and continuing education programs are jointly conducted. The two religious congregations collaborated in writing a single rule of life. Because of these opportunities, the groups are able to bring together laity, clergy and religious to minister as a single unit in the church.

- The Sisters of the Holy Child Jesus are traditionally involved in education. As a result of long-term planning, the congregation was able to predict available personnel for the next two decades. Realizing that the sisters will not be able to meet their current educational commitments, the provincial council embarked on a program of collaboration with the lay boards of the schools. Together they established a structure to identify the specific values which the sisters brought to the schools and determine how these values could be sustained even when the sisters are no longer present.

- The Oblates of Mary Immaculate are in the process of creating opportunities and structures for making collaboration a reality. In a number of provinces in the United States they offer workshops on collaboration, lay ministry, lay leadership and spirituality. These programs are attended by congregation members and their lay associates in ministry.

- Until a few years ago almost all continuing education programs for clergy were restricted to clergy. Today more dioceses, like the Diocese of Cleveland, open many of their programs to laity and non-ordained religious. In our experience, the sessions that combine clergy, laity and religious are the most stimulating and successful ones. When the opportunities for dialogue are available, many fantasies and stereotypes which interfere with meaningful collaboration are dispelled.

This chapter has offered some general principles that foster collaboration as well as several examples of collaboration in action. There are many more situations where collaboration is a reality. We hope that in your own ministry you have made these basic decisions for collaboration: We should; we want to; we can; we will.